THE
TAROT
COURT CARDS

THE
TAROT
COURT CARDS

Archetypal Patterns of Relationship
in the Minor Arcana

KATE WARWICK-SMITH

Destiny Books
Rochester, Vermont

Destiny Books
One Park Street
Rochester, Vermont 05767
www.InnerTraditions.com

Destiny Books is a division of Inner Traditions International

Library of Congress Cataloging-in-Publication Data

Warwick-Smith, Kate, 1959-
   The tarot court cards : archetypal patterns of relationship in the
minor arcana / Kate Warwick-Smith.
      p. cm.
Includes bibliographical references.
   ISBN 0-89281-092-0
   1. Minor arcana (Tarot) I. Title.
   BF1879.T2W37 2003
   133.3'2424—dc21

                              2002156219

Printed and bound in the United States at Lake Book Manufacturing, Inc.

10 9 8 7 6 5 4 3 2 1

Text design and layout by Priscilla Baker

This book was typeset in Legacy with Black Chancery as the display typeface.

For Simon

Contents

Tables

Acknowledgments

In the lengthy process of writing this book, I have benefited from the contributions of many people. I would like to acknowledge Susan Bassett, Kimberly Bess, Batja Cates, Dennis Daniels (in memory), Robin Fife, Gay Kisby, Arisha Wenneson, deTraci Regula, and Lindsay Whiting for their enthusiasm and feedback during the beginning stages of this project. For later editorial help and insight, thanks are due to Timothy Campbell, Stephen Grafenstine, Karen Misuraca, and Joanie Springer. As I hunted down various bits and pieces of needed information, I benefited from the gracious and magnanimous assistance of Krys Bottrill, Peter Cawley, Michael Cooper, Ina Custers, Laura Lazzelle, John McLeod, and Simon Wintle. I am indebted to Michael Bess for his translation help with *Le Tarot Divinatoire* and Chrysalis Counseling Services for Women for providing a quiet writing sanctuary when I needed it most.

I owe thanks, meals, and much, much more to understanding family and valued friends: Shelley T. Daniels, Elise Dwyer, Barrie Elrod, Kerianne Hohener, Julie McGee, and Tubby Smith. I would also like to extend my sincere thanks to Dolores Ashcroft-Nowicki, Chris Corey, Roberta Goldfarb, and Devin Ryder, who each provided key support along the way. In addition, I could not have done this without the inspiring influence of my students and clients and the stalwart encouragement of Ned Atchison.

Finally, my love and profound gratitude go to Simon, Bo, and Shona Warwick-Smith.

Introduction

This book reveals a new way to interpret the sixteen court cards of the Tarot deck, a method that offers valuable insight into our personal relationships.

The core idea presented in the following pages is that the "face cards" of the Tarot depict people in our lives who support us in unique ways. Traditionally the kings, queens, knights, and pages of the Tarot deck are defined as the interpersonal aspect, the "people cards," representing people around us or personality traits within us. Modern court card interpretations, though, are often idiosyncratic, confusing, and difficult to apply in a practical way. However, when the court cards are viewed through the lens of this book, they can clearly and accurately reveal the nature of a support-based relationship between the querent (the person asking the question of the Tarot) and someone in the querent's life.

The evidence that court cards point to our supporters can be gleaned from some of the earliest references to European card playing, where the game is called the Game of Deputies. The word *deputies* refers to the court cards, and a deputy is defined as an assistant, a representative appointed to carry out a specific job. The phrase *a game of deputies* gives us our first clue as to the significance of these cards on a divinatory level. It hints that court cards may represent people who, while maybe not consciously elected allies, are clearly part of our support team. The Game of Deputies aptly and colorfully reflects the theme of this book.

From Native American traditions that hold spirit ally relationships as all-important, to the New Age Michael teachings that refer to support circles, spiritual traditions old and new speak of support as an important aspect of personal growth and good health. The early rival to Christianity, Gnosticism, propounds the "call from without," indicating a spiritually important supportive relationship. In addition, the Chinese I Ching consistently points to various types of relationships and frequently advises that the querent seek his or her family of support. And just outside the realm of spirituality, modern psychotherapeutic practice looks closely at a person's support network.

Ten years ago, in the wake of studying a number of these spiritual traditions and puzzling over how to interpret court cards while giving Tarot readings, a light bulb went on for me. I realized that the Tarot might be one more tradition that embodies the perennial concept of support. At that time I jotted down a few notes. Several years later I put pen to paper to flesh out those ideas and to see if using the theoretical basis of the Qabalah could help describe archetypal patterns of relationship that these other spiritual traditions suggest. I discovered that the inherent structure and symbolism of the court cards, whether by design or accident, implied a set of congruent ideas centered around supportive relationships. This discovery gave birth to a method of court card interpretation that was both insightful and accurate.

During the initial writing process, I showed the manuscript to a few people, yet for a good number of years it sat incubating. Meanwhile I trained in the field of counseling psychology. Then, in an odd twist of fate, the manuscript found its way to a publisher.

As I began final revisions, it seemed that my clients were describing their relationships as if they had read my manuscript. They spoke of their disappointment in not receiving support while growing up, such as the Unconditional Love (King of Cups), Trust (Knight of Pentacles), or Compassion (Queen of Cups) of a parent. Instead they experienced the Abuser (Queen of Pentacles), Betrayer (King of Cups), Victim (Queen of Cups), or Critic (Queen of Swords). They also described important supportive relationships that were empowering and life changing, such as Protector (Knight of Pentacles), Champion (Knight of Swords), Adviser (King of Swords), or Spiritual Elder (King of Wands).

The court cards had made their way into my counseling office. Or perhaps they had always been there and I was just beginning to spot them. It did not take long for me to realize that *every relationship we have can be described in terms of support.* Whether positive, negative, long-term, or short-term, every relationship is some form of support. This is a big statement to make. But taken alongside the teachings of Eastern spiritual leaders and Western environmentalists that all planetary life is interconnected, support can be seen as the thread in the web of connection.

Some may ask, but how can a "negative relationship" be defined as support? Support has many facets. People help us in positive ways (supporters) or challenge us by providing obstacles to be overcome or "lessons" to be learned in the form of difficult or "negative" relationships (detractors). And sometimes we pay for support, such as with a consultant, tutor, babysitter, personal trainer, or therapist. Unfortunately we live in a society where asking for or receiving support is often seen as weakness or lack of ability. One goal of this book is to open up the world of support to reveal exactly who supports us, how they support us, and how we can bring more of that into our lives. This knowledge can be life changing.

A second goal of this book is to demonstrate how the court cards can reflect our inner life. People in our external world can mirror an inner process. In psychological jargon this is called projection, where we notice characteristics in someone else that in truth belong to us. We are unaware of these aspects of ourselves and see them instead in another person. We can usually tell that projection is happening when we react strongly to a person. So it follows that the court cards, as well as representing people in our lives, can reflect our own personality characteristics, inner figures, or subpersonalities that enhance (resource) or hinder (challenge) our efforts in the world. This book provides tools for examining those parts of ourselves.

For those who are interested in the divinatory aspect of the court cards, *The Tarot Court Cards* lays out simple and useful methods of interpretation. In addition, for students of the Western Mysteries, meditation techniques and pathworkings for exploring these cards are included.

NOTES ON GENDER, DUALITY, AND TERMINOLOGY

Gender: Any term or role that is matched with a court card, such as Mentor with the King of Pentacles, may be interpreted as either male or female. Even though the traditional court card titles of king, queen, knight, and page suggest gender, I see this as a description of focus rather than gender. For example, kings might be described as more outwardly focused, while queens might be described as more inwardly focused. Men and women possess both of those qualities. Therefore, a king or a queen may represent either a male or a female.

Duality versus continuum: This book often describes the positive and negative attributes of the court cards in a dualistic, black-and-white fashion. For example, as a positive inner resource the King of Cups is Unconditional Love, and as an inner challenge it is Hatred. The aim here is to show the extremes of a spectrum that is in truth a continuum rather than a stark dichotomy. So, when drawing on the interpretations that I suggest, it is important to be aware and make use of shades of meaning.

Terminology: I have provided specific descriptive words for each of the court cards, such as Mentor, Exactor, or Idol. These words are my attempt to describe the court card support function suggested by the Qabalah and elemental symbolism. You may find other words that capture the nuances of a particular court card as it applies to your life.

HOW TO USE THIS BOOK

The first four chapters of this book examine the symbolism, structure, and history of the court cards. We see how the core symbols of royalty and family affirm the idea that court cards can represent support-based relationships. We also see in the historical progression of court card interpretation how this idea is a natural extension of traditional interpretation. Chapter 4 further delineates the unique approach presented in this book using Qabalistic principles to define the court card support roles and their attributes.

The second four chapters describe in detail the qualities of each court card as supporters, detractors, resources, and challenges while also showing a range of traditional interpretations. The final chapters present ways the information can be used in readings and explored via divination, personal process, meditation, pathworking, and magical technique.

The appendix has a useful one-page summary of the court card roles and a quick reference guide that briefly describes the qualities of the various roles of the court cards. You may also refer to the glossary for definitions of any unfamiliar terms.

You may wish to begin using the relationship approach to interpreting court cards immediately, without delving into its historical and conceptual underpinnings. In that case, I suggest you read chapter 4, "A Qabalistic Equation," then skip to chapter 9, "Divination with Court Cards," while using chapters 5 through 8 as your interpretive guide. For those of you who like to read from the beginning of a book, the journey starts with the royal dynasties of ancient Egypt.

A NOTE ABOUT THE ARTWORK

The court card images accompanying the text are primarily drawn from the Rider Waite Tarot deck designed by Arthur E. Waite and Pamela Coleman Smith. This deck was chosen because it has become the standard from which other decks are designed, and it symbolically captures the essence of the occult Tarot. Additional court cards from other popular decks are also represented, to show how the ideas presented in this book are reflected in a diverse array of Tarot images. The Rider-Waite court cards are presented without captions, because they are easily identified by the title appearing on the card itself. Court card illustrations from other decks are captioned for easier card identification and to indicate the deck from which they were chosen.

ONE
The Royal Family

Royalty and family, the core symbolism suggested by the Tarot court cards, point to two fundamental human drives: to seek relationship with the divine and to live and evolve within community. The symbol of royalty is represented on the face cards by the designation of king, queen, knight, and page. The symbol of family is shown in the grouping of man, woman, young man, and child or sometimes daughter.

A glimpse into this symbolic foundation sets the stage for understanding the court cards' essential message. In the following pages we look at royalty, its social role since ancient times and its symbolic significance, to show how the court cards link us to our divinity and to inner resources of strength. We then consider the first grouping of people that we belong to, family, as a symbol for community to demonstrate how the court cards link us to a core group of relationships.

THE HIGH PRIESTESS

ROYALTY: OUR CONNECTION TO DIVINITY

Monarchy is an ancient social institution found in many cultures. Its history is by far older and more widespread than that of its democratic cousin, republican government, and dates at least to the Egyptian Old Kingdom of nearly five thousand years ago.

In the distant past, royalty connected us with the divine. Ancient Egyptians believed that their earliest kings were gods and that their later kings at least carried the line of divinity within them.[1] In ancient Mesopotamia, the New Year was brought in by the sacred marriage, the heiros gamos, of the king (representative of the people) with the high priestess (representative of the Goddess). Beltane, a spring ceremony of northern Europe, had a similar theme. In these societies people relied on royalty to mediate between them and the gods to ensure the continuation of the community. They believed that having a divine presence in a king went a long way toward ensuring bountiful harvests and success in war.

On the social side, in these pre-Hellenistic times human consciousness was at a communal level. People identified first with family, clan, community, and land. Social and geographic groupings were in turn tied to a specific deity or set of deities. For example, in Egypt major towns each had a god or goddess who was the principal divinity for that region. In Greece the city of Athens was associated with the goddess Athena. This communal consciousness was also deeply attuned to the spiritual level of life.

Only secondarily did people identify themselves as separate and individual. David Ulansey, author of "Cultural Transition and Spiritual Transformation: From Alexander the Great to Cyberspace," writes: "Up until the Hellenistic period, the structure of one's identity was centered in the group—tribe, polis, nation—of which one was a member. This does not mean, of course, that people were entirely unaware of their own individuality, but it is the case that the sense of belonging to a group was decisively more in the foreground of consciousness than it is today."[2] Dr. Ulansey cites as an example that prior to the Hellenization of the Mediterranean, fear of a personal death was minimized by the belief in the continuation of the community. And as we know, common belief presumed that community endured via the royal leader's connection to divinity.

After Alexander the Great conquered the Mediterranean (fourth century B.C.E.), a mixing and intermingling of this vast network of communities began. By necessity communal consciousness gave way to a growing personal awareness because of the movement and displacement of great numbers of people and the loss of a "collective identity,"[3] which already had been in transition for some time.[4] Now many individuals' connection with the divine was no longer tied specifically to their community, to the land, or to its royal figures. A personal search for a new spiritual connection became imperative. This development gave rise to religious cults as a new type of community that transcended place. Religions such as Mithraism, Gnosticism, and the Mysteries of Isis, among others, became widespread and filled this need. For example, one could travel from Egypt to western Europe and find temples dedicated to Isis all along the way. This new type of religion-based community provided a means to connect with the gods outside of a geographical context and took over the royal mediating function, providing a way for people to connect with the divine.

Traditional and nontraditional religious groups continue today in this vein. Most modern pagan, Wiccan, and Hermetic groups, as well as Christian, Buddhist, Judaic, and Islamic sects, have no specific connection to a geographical location. For example, as a Catholic you can go to many churches throughout the world and feel a sense of cohesion and belonging. Religious leaders such as the pope and the Dalai Lama, however, continue to fill a royalty-like mediating function for many people. And despite the rise of democratic leadership throughout the world, the archetype of royalty is still deeply embedded in the contemporary psyche. Witness the extraordinary global outpouring of sympathy and the sense of bereavement over the unexpected death of Britain's Princess Diana.

Nonetheless, the notion of royalty has gradually taken on a growing symbolic function, both exoterically and esoterically. We perhaps see the beginnings of this in the Gnostic "Hymn of the Pearl" from the third century B.C.E., where the metaphor of royalty suggests the higher spiritual self, a personal divinity.

In this delightful and profound story the prince has been sent to Egypt to retrieve the pearl of wisdom. After recovering it, he returns to the kingdom of his father to assume once again his robes of royalty. He declares, "As I now beheld the robe, it seemed to me suddenly to become a mirror-image of myself: myself entire I saw in it, and it entire I saw in myself, that we were two in separateness, and yet again one in the sameness of our forms . . . and the image of the King of kings was depicted all over it."[5] The royal robe had transformed to reflect an inner divinity or higher self.

Symbolically, the robe or garment in the Gnostic context can also "denote the body as a passing earthly form encasing the soul. . . . A garment is donned and doffed and changed, the earthly garment for that of light."[6] The garment, or body, is but a physical sheath that wraps an incorporeal light. The robes of the Tarot court figures likewise clothe an inner divinity. Interestingly, the term *court card* is an adaptation of *coat card,* an earlier name used to describe these cards.[7]

Later alchemical mandalas and writings echo the symbolic connection between royalty and an inner divinity, such as Salomon Trismosin's *Splendor Solis:* "The sun shone brightly, and in it came a consummation: the king in all his glory, rescued and renewed, richly adorned and altogether comely."[8] Commentator Adam McLean interprets the king in this parable and accompanying mandala as the alchemist's soul as it is transformed and reborn. We then find that this idea of personal divinity symbolized by royalty is expressed in the Tarot as well, through major arcana and court card symbolism.

So far our journey into the past has demonstrated how the royal court of the Tarot reflects an ancient communal consciousness linking us to our divinity and to our tribe. Next we will see how the fam-

Splendor Solis Emblem 7

ily model suggested by the court cards also connects us to a community of support and to inner sources of power and knowing.

FAMILY: OUR LINK TO COMMUNITY

Tarot court cards form a complete family system of a father (king), mother (queen), son (knight), and daughter (page or maiden). In 1889 an early writer on the Tarot, Papus, compared the four royals to a family unit. He related the king, queen, knight, and page to man, woman, young man, and child. He states that they are "the same symbols applied to the family as the four great principles applied to humanity, and to know them in one case is to know them in the other."[9]

Family is usually our first community and our primary support system. Family ushers us into the world and may help us to exit it as well. When psychotherapists assess a client's strengths, part of their assessment includes looking at the client's support system. Does the client have people he or she can call on for help? Sometimes the support system does not include family members but rather friends or local communities such as church groups or gatherings of people that share a common interest—women's support groups, business networking groups, or support groups for alcoholics. Modern communication and transportation have made it easier for people to gather in groups like these.

While the proliferation and specialization of support groups may be a trend, the support group in and of itself is not new. Recalling royalty, nearly every king or queen has made good use of an inner court of support. King Arthur had his knights of the Round Table, Robin Hood his band of merry men, and Jesus his twelve disciples. Today the president of the United States has the Cabinet, and corporation presidents have their boards of directors. In these "support groups" each member is perceived as an ally in one way or another. When you think about it, we all have some version of an inner court—people we rely on to help us in various ways in our lives. How many of us give it much thought? Do we know exactly who they are and how they support us? And do we know how we in turn support them?

The course that began at least two millennia ago, away from communal consciousness toward a focus on individual identity, continues. Modern technology enables both more independence, on the one hand, and the possibility for relationships with a wider range of people, on the other. However, the intimate relationships of a closely bound community are harder to come by. We have gained greater individual freedom at the risk of experiencing greater alienation. As individuals trying to come to terms with our place in this complex world, it is even more important to recognize, use, and value the personal relationships around us by acknowledging our "true tribe" or the select community that supports us. Within the Tarot, the court card "family" represents this tribe.

ROYAL FAMILY MEMBERS AS ARCHETYPES

Court cards, though, have both outer and inner faces. The twentieth-century psychoanalyst Carl Jung spoke of the family system in terms of archetypes within the individual psyche. He named these inner constellations of consciousness the Great Father (or Wise Old Man), the Great Mother, the Divine Child, and the Divine Maiden.

The correlation between these archetypes and the four court cards is readily apparent. To very briefly characterize them: the Great Father

The Quaternity of Elements: Earth, Air, Water, Fire—
The World,
Alchemical Tarot

and kings equal authority, the Great Mother and queens equal nourishment, the Divine Child and knights equal independence, and the Divine Maiden and pages equal innocence or vulnerability.

These figures, king, queen, knight, and page, also compose a quaternity, a grouping of four. Four is a symbol of wholeness and within Jungian psychology denotes the central archetype of the Self: "The quaternity is a more or less direct representation of the God who is manifest in his creation."[10] Again, the number symbolism inherent in the Tarot court echoes what we have heard before, that the court cards speak of an inner resource (archetype) of great power and divinity that is multifaceted, or shall we say, multifaced.

What of this inner divinity? What is its function and how does it speak through the court cards? Recalling "The Hymn of the Pearl" the Tarot royalty might be likened to the family of the prince (a foursome, by the way). While the prince is in Egypt struggling to regain the pearl, his family sends him a letter awakening him from a debilitating slumber. The wise words of his family (his supporters) remind him of who he is and of his purpose, providing the key that leads to his success. Like him, we are not alone. In later chapters the court cards reveal themselves as sources of outer support and inner strength.

FROM DIVINITY TO DIVINATION

The leap from speaking of royalty and divinity to speaking of the history of court card divination may seem a large one. Yet the gap may not be as wide as we think, for the bridge appears in the words themselves—*divinity* and *divination*. Divination is our attempt to seek connection and communication with the divine and has a history all its own.

TWO
From Arrow Divination to a Game of Deputies
A Court Card History

Divination is an age-old practice that has enlisted the help of a diverse array of objects, including arrows, entrails, tea leaves, stars, palms, sticks, stones, bones, ashes, the weather, and, last but not least, playing cards. Treatises on the origin of playing cards frequently treat the Tarot (as used for divination) as an aside in the history of playing cards. In good part this is owing to evidence suggesting that Tarot, or Tarrochi, cards were first used as game playing cards and only later as a tool for divination. Divination with cards is generally viewed as an outgrowth of this earlier development.

However, Catherine Hargrave, in her book *A History of Playing Cards,* turns the tables. She proposes instead that games such as cards are the offspring of ancient divinatory systems.[1] We may never know exactly which came first, card games or divination. Nonetheless, when we dig further into the history of cards, we discover that divination and games, each a folk art in its own right, may indeed be closely linked.

ARROW DIVINATION (BELOMANCY)

Mr. Stewart Culin, a playing card authority of the early twentieth century, believed that chess and cards "derived from the divinatory use of the arrow."[2] While some of his theories about playing card origins have been disproved by recent discoveries, his belief in arrow divination—belomancy—as a precursor to card games, and by association the Tarot, is intriguing.

The arrow was first used by humans in the late Paleolithic period and was employed throughout the world with only a few isolated exceptions. Belomancy seems to have been practiced widely by such diverse groups as Native Americans, Greeks, Arabs, Tibetans, Chaldeans, and Koreans. We even find references to belomancy in the Bible: "For the king of Babylon has halted at the fork where these two roads diverge, to take the omens. He has shaken the arrows, questioned the teraphim, inspected the liver" (Ezek. 21:20–21).

Arrow divination took different forms. Sometimes an arrow was assigned a direction, such as north, south, right, or left, or choice such as "yes," "no," or "stay home." Then several arrows were shot and the farthest arrow carried the portent. Legend has it that Robin Hood, upon his deathbed, used a similar method by shooting an arrow to mark his final resting spot. Travelers might also toss an arrow in the air; as it fell, the direction it pointed determined the direction of travel. An arrow was also chosen or "shaken" from the quiver to obtain an answer. And some arrow divination practices required the diviner to draw a magic circle, then toss arrows within the circle.[3]

While no direct evidence clearly links games such as cards with arrow divination, modern games like darts (tossing arrows into a circle), picking straws (shaking an arrow from a holder), spinning the bottle to select a partner (tossing an arrow into the air to determine a direction of travel), and divination tools such as I Ching yarrow sticks offer provocative comparisons. In addition, our descriptive language of the Tarot further suggests a remote connection to arrow divination—we "pull" a card (arrow) and "throw" a spread (arrow).

ASIAN CARDS

Early playing cards from Korea may be our best evidence that links arrow divination to playing cards. Korean cards are very long and narrow and have an arrow feather (fletch) painted on the back of each one. The earliest Korean cards in existence have eight suits with ten cards in each suit. The "court card" is the tenth card and is called the general.

Chinese cards, believed by some to have been derived from Korean cards, vary in size, shape, and number of suits but also have ten cards per suit, with the tenth card being a court card. Chinese suits—Coins, Strings of Coins, and Myriads of Strings of Coins—bear a faint resemblance to modern European suits and may be a distant relative. What is most interesting, though, about the Chinese cards is the three extra cards that are added to the deck, the White Flower, the Red Flower, and the Old Thousand. These cards differ from the others by their portrayal of characters from "The Story of the River's Banks," a Chinese folktale.[4] One wonders if a parallel can be drawn to the Tarot Fool and his archetypal journey through life as depicted in the remaining twenty-one cards of the major arcana. Speculation aside, the next point on our playing card time line is Arabia, where apparently new suits evolved and new games developed.

ARABIC CARDS

European playing cards are generally believed to be directly descended from Arabic playing cards brought to Europe from the Mamluk empire of Egypt. Remnants of these Arabic cards date to the thirteenth century. They have four suits—swords, polo sticks, cups, and coins—numbered one through ten, with three additional court cards called *malik* (King), *na'ib malik* (Deputy King), and *thani na'ib* (Second Deputy). The striking similarities between early European cards and the Arabic deck, plus the appearance of cards in Europe in the fourteenth century subsequent to the dating of the Mamluk fragments strongly suggests an Arabic origin.

King of Coins,
Mamluk Deck

Linguistics further supports this hypothesis. The Italian word *naibbe* and the Spanish word *naipes* translate as "cards," or, in fact, as "the Game of Deputies,"[5] and both words may derive from the Arabic word *na'ib* found in the court card titles of the Mamluk cards. The Arabic court cards did not portray human figures for religious reasons but instead were reminiscent of designs found on woven carpets.

EUROPEAN ADAPTATIONS

European card makers altered Arabic court card design by depicting human royal figures. Today these three court cards of the regular playing deck are shown as king, queen, and jack. Tarot card packs (as opposed to the regular card deck) contain even further distinctions. Tarot decks incorporate four instead of three courts and contain twenty-two additional cards that serve as a permanent suit of trumps. This extra suit played an important role in ancient Tarot games and later became known as the major arcana (greater mysteries) of the occult Tarot.

The earliest Tarot packs come from the period of the Visconti-Sforza Tarot around 1415. Then, over the next hundred years, Tarot decks proliferated and became well known all over Europe. Historical evidence suggests that Tarot cards were first used for playing trick-taking games, similar to modern games such as bridge or whist. Variations of these medieval Tarot games remain popular to this day.

Specifically designed occult Tarot decks did not appear for another three hundred years. Since then the divinatory use of the Tarot has given rise to an abundance of artistically unique decks.

Generally, occult Tarot decks like Tarot game playing decks are composed of three divisions. In the occult Tarot forty cards (ten cards to each of four suits) compose the minor arcana (the lesser mysteries). The suits are commonly known as wands, cups, swords, and pentacles. In addition the minor arcana include sixteen court cards (four courts to a suit), namely the king, queen, knight, and page. Finally, the major arcana (the greater mysteries) compose the remainder of the deck totaling twenty-two cards numbered 0 to 21. Each major arcana card bears a unique title such as Fool, Magician, or Devil.

King of Wands,
Visconti-Sforza Tarot

Despite their structural similarities, occult Tarot cards and Tarot game playing cards obviously differ considerably in usage and meaning. However, might there exist a connection between how a Tarot card was originally valued as a game piece and then later perceived in a divinatory capacity? If so, curiosity leads us to wonder how the court cards were used in Tarot-based games. Could this give us a clue as to their earliest divinatory meanings?

In modern Tarot games the major arcana continues to act as a permanent trump suit. At the end of the game, scoring is by point rather than by trick. In this system the court cards possess a high point value, and only the Fool, the Magician, and the World of the major arcana score the same as or higher than the King in the court cards. The other three court cards also possess point value, whereas none of the other major or minor arcana do. In other words the major arcana possess power as trumps but have little scoring value when compared with the court cards. This is interesting to think of in terms of Tarot divination, where today major arcana cards have more perceived value than the courts or other minor arcana cards. This may not always have been so. However, writings on the divinatory Tarot before the eighteenth century offer scant information, even though these cards may have been used in that capacity as much as two hundred years earlier. And as we see in the next chapter, the passage of two hundred years can significantly change the way cards are interpreted.

Why do we interpret court cards the way we do? Just as playing cards and Tarot cards have a developmental history, so does court card interpretation. In the next chapter we examine how the meaning of court cards has developed over time.

Date	Person	Place	Event	Significance
Ca. 2000 B.C.E.		Mesopotamia, Anatolia, Egypt, Canaan	Arrow divination practiced	Possible ancestor to modern playing cards and the Tarot for divination
not known		Korea	"Fighting Strips," narrow cards that bear the mark of an arrow on the back	Korean card design suggests they may be derived from the Korean practice of the divinatory arrow
969 C.E.	Emperor Mu-tsung and his wives	China	Legend states that the emperor played cards with his wives for their amusement	Cards may exist in China at this early date
250–1517		Arabia: Egyptian Mamluk empire	Cards for playing games used with four suits and three court cards per suit	These cards predate European cards and appear to be their nearest ancestor
1300		Europe	Paper mills began to proliferate	Cards became a more feasible alternative to other types of games, especially for nobility
1371		Spain	Cards (naip) mentioned in Catalan document	First mention of cards in Europe
1377	John of Rheinfelden (Swiss monk)	Bern, Switzerland	Playing cards mentioned in legal documents	More detailed description of playing cards given
1392	Gringonneur	France	Gringonneur designed decks for France's King Charles VI	Seventeen cards in the Bibliothèque Nationale may be later copies of these decks; if so, they had Tarot trumps

KEY EVENTS IN THE HISTORY OF THE TAROT (continued)

Date	Person	Place	Event	Significance
1415		Italy	Visconti-Sforza Tarot deck	Oldest surviving Tarot deck
1450		Europe	Renaissance begins	A period of "revival of learning." New social and intellectual climate affected how Tarot cards were used and perceived.
1500		Germany	Wood-block printing developed	Made reproduction of Tarot and books easier and more widely available
1517	Johann Reuchlin	Germany	Published *On the Art of the Kabbalah*	First non-Jew to write on the Kabbalah,* emphasizing its usefulness to Christians
1533	Henry Cornelius Agrippa	Cologne, Germany	Published *Three Books of Occult Philosophy*	Incorporated Reuchlin's view of the Kabbalah into Western magic
1540	Francesco Marcolino	Italy	*Le Sorti* published	Earliest known printed reference to divination using playing cards
1616	Unknown	Germany	Three Rosicrucian manifestos published: *Fama Fraternis, Confessio Fraternita, Chemical Wedding of Christian Rosenkreutz*	Mentions "Book T" (presumably the Tarot), linking the Tarot with Hermeticism
1748	Grimaud	France	Tarot of Marseilles deck produced	Ancestor to the modern Tarot deck
1781	Court de Gebelin	France	*Le Monde Primitif* published	Claims that the Tarot came from ancient Egypt

Date	Person	Place	Event	Significance
1785	Etteilla	France	*How to Entertain Yourself with the Deck of Cards Called Tarot* published	First book to give a detailed look at Tarot divination
1856	Eliphas Lévi	France	*Transcendental Magic* published	Links the major arcana of the Tarot with the 22 letters of the Hebrew alphabet; assigns elements to the suits
1886	Dr. Wynn Westcott, Dr. Woodfort, Dr. Woodman	London, England	Occult society, the Hermetic Order of the Golden Dawn, founded	A culmination of the last 400 years integrates Renaissance magic, Hermeticism, Kabbalah, and the Tarot into the modern tradition of Western magic
1910	Arthur E. Waite and Pamela Colman Smith	London, England	Rider-Waite Tarot deck published	Became widely popular; many modern decks modeled upon this one
1944	Aleister Crowley. Tarot images illustrated by Lady Frieda Harris	England	*The Book of Thoth* published in a limited edition	The book contained newly designed Tarot images; this now-popular deck was not widely available until after 1969

* I use Qabalah to refer to Hermetic mysticism and Kabbalah to refer to Judaic mysticism.

Sources: *The Encyclopedia of Tarot*, Stuart R. Kaplan; *A History of Playing Cards*, Catherine Perry Hargrave; *The Oxford Guide to Card Games*, David Parlett; *The Qabalistic Tarot*, Robert Wang; *The Tarot*, Alfred Douglas; *Tarot for Your Self*, Mary K. Greer; *The Tarot Handbook*, Angeles Arrien.

THREE
Two Hundred Years of Court Card Interpretation

This chapter shows various ways court cards have been interpreted over time, from broad communal or worldly interpretations, such as "matters only settled by war,"[1] to interpretations relating more specifically to individuals, such as "an older man or older mastery of passionate thinking and mental determination."[2] The evolution of court card interpretation seems to reflect social developments such as the diminishing role of royalty and the increasing importance placed on personalized growth and individual autonomy.

From the late 1700s (when we have the first detailed account of Tarot divination) to the present day, court card interpretation breaks down into four traditional ways of reading cards:

- As an environmental influence

- As a person (other than the querent) identified by personality type, physique, sex, occupation, or age

- As relating to spirituality: the Qabalah, astrology, I Ching, and other spiritual traditions

- As the querent's inner potential and talents, capacities, psychological state

Each of these categories is amplified below. Then a fifth method of interpretation, identifying one's network of supportive relationships—the theme of this book—is offered:

• As supporter, detractor, resource, and challenge

COURT CARDS AS AN ENVIRONMENTAL INFLUENCE

Examples of court cards indicating an environmental influence come from the French card maker Grimaud, who published the first edition of the Tarot of Marseilles in 1748 and continued to

KING OF COINS

King of Coins,
Tarot of Marseilles

publish variations of this classic deck up through the late twentieth century. Bill Butler in his book *Dictionary of the Tarot* presents court card interpretations attributed to Grimaud. The meanings assigned to the court cards are notable as they often describe an external influence, a societal or cosmic force arising from an individual's environment and not necessarily attached to any specific person. While it is not clear when the Grimaud interpretations originated, this type of interpretation nonetheless recalls to mind a time when royalty held a controlling influence on people's lives. Here are some examples of this type of court card interpretation from Grimaud:

King of Pentacles: The occult and fatal action of cosmic forces, possessions in a precarious state.

Queen of Swords: Calumnious will, unpleasant advise, slander, evil words. Destruction bearing fruit.

Knight of Wands: Providential aid, support given in everything, protection, support and strength brought by the unknown.

Page of Cups: Spiritual and moral riches offered as a reward.[3]

COURT CARDS AS A TYPE OF PERSON

At about the same time that the *Tarot of Marseilles* was published, a Frenchman by the name of Alliette (pen name Etteilla) was making a name for himself by publishing the first book on Tarot divination, *How to Entertain Yourself with the Deck of Cards Called Tarot.* Etteilla also later published the first esoteric deck specifically designed with divination in mind. Etteilla's court card interpretations mostly describe personality characteristics, physical characteristics, age, and occupation.

The beginnings of this type of interpretation may not have originated with Etteilla but may have evolved much earlier (in the 1400s), when court cards were depicted in playing card decks as specific rulers. For example, the King of Hearts (Cups) was sometimes named Charlemagne and the King of Diamonds (Swords), Caesar. It is a small step from this to associating the cards with a specific type of person. Court card interpretations relating to someone with a specific personality, with a characteristic appearance, or of a certain age may have developed from this early type of comparison.

Here are some of Etteilla's interpretations of the court cards as found in Papus's *Le Tarot Divinatoire:*

King of Pentacles: Dark Man. This card with regard to the medicine of the spirit signifies in its upright position: a dark man, shopkeeper, businessman, merchant, banker, stockbroker, accountant, gambler. Physics, geometry, mathematics, science. Teacher, professor, scholar. Reversed: Vice, fault, weakness, defectiveness, unorthodox, imperfect disposition. Debauchery, baseness, ugliness, deformed, corrupt.

Queen of Swords: Widow. This card with regard to the medicine of the spirit signifies in its upright position: widowhood, loss, absence, famine, dearth, barren, destitute, poverty. Empty, vacant, unoccupied, unemployed, idle, free. Reversed: Wicked woman, malignant, malicious, deceit, trickery, artifice. Mischievousness, bigotry, prudery, hypocrisy.

Knight of Wands: Departure. This card with regard to the medicine of the spirit signifies in its upright position: departure, traveling, banishment, separation, absence, abandonment, change, evasion, escape, desertion, emigration. Transposition. Reversed: disunity, fight, parting, dissension, division, split, separation. Quarrel, dispute, break, fracture, discontinuation, interruption.

Page of Cups: Blond Boy. This card with regard to the medicine of the spirit signifies in its upright position: blond boy, studious, diligent, observant, considerate, contemplative, employed. Reversed: inclined toward passion, affection, attachment, taste, friendship. Heart, desire, wanting, attraction, engagement, seduction, invitation, agreement. Jealousy, seduction, flattery, fawning, praise.[4]

A hundred years after Etteilla made his debut, MacGregor Mathers, an early member of the Golden Dawn society, published *The Tarot.* His court card interpretations share similarities with Etteilla's, though exhibiting a flavor of the nonspecific environmental influence, as in the examples below.

King of Pentacles: Dark man, victory, bravery, courage, success. An old and vicious man, a dangerous man, doubt, fear, peril, danger.

Queen of Swords: Widowhood, loss, privation, absence, separation. A bad woman, ill-tempered and bigoted, riches and discord, abundance together with worry, joy with grief.

Knight of Wands: Departure, separation, disunion. Rupture, discord, quarrel.

Page of Cups: A fair youth, confidence, probity, discretion, integrity. A flatterer, deception, artifice.[5]

About a year after Mathers's book came out, Papus, also known as Gerard Encausse, published *Tarot of the Bohemians*. His court card interpretations follow a similar pattern, although varying considerably in places from Mathers's.

King of Pentacles: A fair man, inimical or indifferent.

Queen of Swords: A dark, wicked woman. The card also indicates her actions, gossip, and calumnies.

Knight of Wands: A dark young man, a friend.

Page of Cups: A fair child. A messenger. Birth.[6]

Still within this genre, twenty years later Arthur E. Waite, author of *The Pictorial Key to the Tarot* and cocreator of the Rider-Waite Tarot, laid out his expanded court card interpretations, examples of which follow.

KNIGHT of WANDS.

King of Pentacles: Valor, realizing intelligence, business and normal intellectual aptitude, sometimes mathematical gifts and attainments of this kind, success in these paths. Reversed: vice, weakness, ugliness, perversity, corruption, peril.

Queen of Swords: Widowhood, female sadness and embarrassment, absence, sterility, mourning, privation, separation. Reversed: malice, bigotry, artifice, prudery, bale, deceit.

Knight of Wands: Departure, absence, flight, emigration. A dark young man, friendly. Change of residence. Reversed: rupture, division, interruption, discord.

Page of Cups: Fair young man, one impelled to render service and with whom the querent will be connected, a studious youth, news, messages, application, reflection, meditation, the same conditions directed toward business. Reversed: taste, inclination, attachment, seduction, deception, artifice.[7]

Our last example within this category is from Tarot teacher and writer Eden Gray. In 1970 her *Complete Guide to the Tarot* was published. Her interpretations of the court cards clearly build on earlier tradition; however, she adds a personal element, making them more accessible to the general user.

King of Pentacles: This is the chief of industry, a banker, or an owner of large estates. He is a reliable married man and a mathematician with great financial gifts. The card can also betoken a steady temperament, slow to anger; success where money matters are concerned and reliability.

Queen of Swords: A subtle, keen, and quick-witted woman who may represent a widow or one who is unable to bear children. Perhaps she is mourning for those she loves who are far away from her.

Knight of Wands: A young man, possibly a warrior filled with energy. He can be a generous friend or lover but is also likely to be cruel and brutal. He is hasty in all he does. May also mean change of residence, emigration, quick departure.

Page of Cups: A melancholy and passionate youth, studious but given to flights of imagination. Willing to render service to the querent.[8]

Etteilla's groundbreaking work can clearly be seen in the later work of Mathers, Papus, Waite, and Gray. Moreover, this genre of interpretation remains popular to this day.

COURT CARDS ASSUME A SPIRITUAL DIMENSION

Etteilla's influence can also be seen in the category on spirituality. His esoterically designed Tarot deck was the first to connect astro-logical and elemental symbolism to various cards. This practice expanded and gained popularity in the late nineteenth century with the publication of Eliphas Lévi's *Transcendental Magic* in 1856. In this volume Lévi links the Hebrew alphabet to the major arcana of the Tarot and links the four elements (Air, Fire, Water, and Earth) to the suits. This influential volume set the foundation for an expansion of court card interpretations by early-twentieth-century occultists. Using elemental symbolism and follow-ing Lévi in merging compatible

Knight of Disks, Thoth Tarot

occult systems, Paul Foster Case and Aleister Crowley both contributed another layer to court card interpretation, adding mystical qualities and Qabalistic and astrological associations to the now rather standard interpretations. (Only single court card examples are given here from Case and Crowley, respectively, because of their length.)

King of Pentacles: Time period is from the beginning of the last decanate of Sagittarius to the end of the second decanate of Capricorn, from December 12 to January 10. This period combines the rulerships of the Sun, Saturn, and Venus. Well dignified: a dark man, friendly to querent, practical, steady, reliable. Good at practical application. Things prosper and increase under his direction. Slow to anger but furious when aroused. Ill dignified: selfish, animal, material. Has great power of solidifying all evil forces directed against the projects of the querent but is nevertheless somewhat stupid. Appearance: dark hair and dark eyes.[9]

King of Pentacles: Represents the fiery part of Earth and refers in particular to the phenomena of mountains, earthquakes, and gravitation; but it also represents the activity of Earth regarded as the producer of life. He rules from the twenty-first degree of Leo to the twentieth degree of Virgo and is thus concerned greatly with agriculture. This warrior is short and sturdy in type. ... Those whom he symbolizes tend to be dull, heavy, preoccupied with material things. ... They lack initiative; their fire is the smoldering fire of the process of growth. ... If ill dignified, these people are hopelessly stupid, slavish, and quite incapable of foresight even in their own affairs. In the Yi King, the fiery part of Earth is represented by the sixty-second hexagram, *Hsiao Kwo.* ... But it is also suggestive of the geomantic figure Conjunctio, Mercury in Virgo, corresponding very closely indeed with the Fire of Earth attribution in the Qabalistic system.[10]

Lon Milo DuQuette, a contemporary writer on the Tarot and ritual magic, has continued in this vein, relating the court cards to Enochian magic, a system developed by Dr. John Dee and Edward Kelley in the late 1500s to communicate with angelic beings.[11] At the center of this complicated system are five tables called Enochian Tablets each relating to a specific element (Earth, Air, Fire, Water, and Spirit). Each tablet is divided into smaller squares that are further divided into sections some of which contain letters. A prescribed method for reading the letters inscribed on these tablets produces the names of specific angelic entities. Using the appropriate elemental tablet (for example, the Earth tablet for pentacles) Duquette has related specific angelic entities to the various court cards. His contribution has fascinating implications when viewed together with the support-based theme of this book.

COURT CARDS AS
INNER POTENTIAL AND TALENT

In order to understand the origins of court card interpretation as inner potential and talent, we need to step back again to the late nineteenth century. Concurrent with the emergence of the Golden Dawn society, Sigmund Freud was laying the foundations of modern psychology. This new development is important to note with regard to court card interpretation for two reasons. First, the psychological movement begun by Freud emphasized the individual and discovering what differentiated him or her from others. This growing interest in an individual's psychological nature highlights the importance society continued to place on the ordinary person over and above any royal figure or even social structure, such as family and community. The individual was seen in the context of these social structures rather than defined by them.

Second, Carl Jung, a student of Freud, indirectly influenced court card interpretation through his idea of psychological types.

The Jungian classifications of thinking, feeling, sensing, and intuition can clearly be seen in court card interpretations of the last twenty years.

In this period court card meanings also deepened to reflect characteristics, talents, and resources of the individual having the reading (that is, the querent). In other words, rather than court cards representing an influence or person outside the querent, court cards are seen as reflecting the querent's psychological tendencies. Writers on the Tarot, such as Angeles Arrien and Mary K. Greer, among others, offer court card interpretations of this type.

> ***King of Pentacles*** *(Knight of Disks):* Demonstrates the capacity to manifest skills in the outer world in practical, observable ways. . . . He is determined to achieve harvest in the areas of health and finances. The Knight of Disks represents the doctor or healer in the deck, or the financier or investor in the deck. . . . For women, the Knight of Disks can represent the dynamic assertive part of themselves, the inner animus that wants to sustain abundant health and financial well-being. . . . In the months of Capricorn, Virgo, and Taurus, you could experience more well-being and harvest in your life.[12]

> ***King of Pentacles*** *(Fire of Earth):* Established work. The ability to produce and be practical. A manager, financier, or craftsperson. Responsible and trustworthy, yet stubborn and slow to change. A sensualist. Concerned with security and quality. Questions to answer: How are you using your ability to manage your material affairs? Who is trustworthy yet stubborn? How are you being practical and down-to-earth, or who do you know that is? Sample Affirmation: "I acknowledge Mother Earth as the source of my material well-being."[13]

SUPPORT-BASED
COURT CARD INTERPRETATION

In the following pages I describe how court cards can be interpreted as a person with whom we have a specific support-based relationship, such as a Healer, Mentor, or Spiritual Elder. This approach arises from and builds on the core symbolism of the court cards, royalty and family, linking us to community and hence a grouping of people on whom we rely for support. The support-based notion of court card interpretation seems a natural next step in the evolution of approaches to reading these cards. As stated earlier, now more than ever we need to identify and better understand the relationships around us to avoid feelings of alienation that modern society can invite and, on the positive side, make the most of the joy of human connection.

In this support-based method, I call helpful people with whom the querent has relationships *supporters*. The opposite, *detractors,* are people who block by their negative behavior or attitude, such as a Critic, Betrayer, or Victim. Then, following a more traditional psychological approach, I identify inner aspects of the querent, which are counterparts derived from each supporter and detractor. I call these *resources* and *challenges,* respectively. These personal behaviors and attitudes of the querent can either be supportive of his or her goals or self-blocking.

Next we draw on the Qabalah, the foundation of the Western Mysteries, to help us further reveal the faces of the Tarot court and derive specific information about each support position.

FOUR
A Qabalistic Equation

This chapter considers each court card as an equation consisting of a suit—wand, cup, sword, pentacle—combined with a level of royalty: king, queen, knight, page.

We first look at the suits and the life arenas they predominantly symbolize. Then we relate the four worlds of the Qabalah to the royal hierarchy of king, queen, knight, and page to get an idea of the core impulse emanating from each court card level. When the two are combined—the central idea of each suit with the core impulse of each level of royalty—the court cards come to life, representing people with whom we have relationships of very different kinds.

THE WHEEL OF FORTUNE

*The Four Elements Surround
the Universal Wheel of
Transformation—Wheel of
Fortune, Alchemical Tarot*

THE SUITS

One way Western philosophers have sought to explain existence is by dividing it into four realms. Jung writes: "The division of the process

35

Quinta Essentia Engraving of the Humours shows man as the central symbol divided into four

or of the central symbol into four has always existed, beginning with the four sons of Horus, or the four seraphim of Ezekiel, or the birth of the four Aeons from the Metra (uterus) impregnated by the pneuma in Barbelo-Gnosis, or the cross formed by the lightning (snake) in Böhme's system and ending with the tetrameria of the *aopus alchymicum* and its components (the four elements, qualities, stages, etc.)."[1]

Numerous examples of the one divided by four can be found. In the Bible the Book of Genesis begins with the description of the four rivers running out of Eden. The Judaic Kabbalah describes existence in terms of four worlds. There are the four directions, the four basic elements of the early Greek philosophers, the four levels of transformation of the alchemists, the four Jungian functions, and, last but not least, the four suits of the Tarot and the four court card levels.

In 1856 French occultist and writer Eliphas Lévi assigned the four basic elements (Fire, Water, Air, Earth) to the suits. It was only a short time before others followed his lead and a whole system of attributions evolved surrounding the suits and the quadripartite theme. The table of suit correspondence reflects this development.

Here is a closer look at the suits as they are understood today.

SUIT CORRESPONDENCE TABLE

Suit	Wands	Cups	Swords	Pentacles
Direction	South	West	East	North
Season	Summer	Fall	Spring	Winter
Element	Fire	Water	Air	Earth
Body part	Genitals	Heart	Head	Feet
Jungian function	Intuition	Feeling	Thinking	Sensation
Alchemical stage	Rubedo	Citrinitas	Albedo	Nigredo
Astrology sign	Leo Aries Sagittarius	Pisces Cancer Scorpio	Gemini Libra Aquarius	Taurus Capricorn Virgo
Qabalistic world	Atziluth	Briah	Yetzirah	Assiah
Characteristics/ realms of influence	Intuition Vision Creativity Sexuality Spirituality	Emotion Ideals Hopes Relationships Psychic	Intellect Understanding Logic Reason Struggle, Conflict	Money Livelihood Home Health Survival

Wands: Spirit

The wands suit relates to the magician's will and to the element of Fire, the element that best describes the spark of life that animates all of matter. Hence wands represent our capacity for intuition, vision, inner knowing, insight, and deep understanding, especially in areas relating to spirituality and the mysteries of being human. In daily life the suit of wands, as the phallic shape suggests, relates to vitality, creative projects, sexuality, spiritual activities, and work that we have passion for—this may or may not be our career.

Cups: Love

Cups correspond to the element of Water and describe the fluid, feeling level of our existence. The Cup symbolizes the primordial womb which holds and nurtures the essence of hope, desire, and inspiration. This suit relates to our ability to flow with and adapt to the undercurrents of life and be attuned to unconscious processes. Cups may also refer to the emotional milieu of a relationship or strongly held ideals.

Swords: Knowledge

Swords are matched with the element of Air. Some alchemists describe Air as the element that mediates Fire and Water. We see this when fog or rain is formed in the atmosphere as a result of the sun (fire) interacting with physical bodies of water like oceans and lakes. Psychologically and spiritually, the mind seems to take on a similar mediating function between our lower and higher selves. Thus, swords relate to the mental arena, representing our capacity for intellectual understanding, logic, reason, conscious process, and communication. The sword is a weapon that severs and cuts much like the mind does when it analyzes, decides, or tries to make sense of things. Sword Tarot cards often reflect our struggles and conflicts, because by clearing these hurdles we gain knowledge of ourselves and the world.

Pentacles: Power

The element of Earth is matched with the suit of pentacles. Earlier decks such as the Tarot of Marseilles use the coin as an emblem of this suit instead of the pentacle. The coin as a symbol of commerce corresponds neatly to the earthy arena of this suit, which includes career, money, livelihood, home, possessions, and physical health. The pentacle is a more complex symbol that begs explanation. As its picture suggests, a pentacle is a wooden or metal disk with a painted or en-

graved pentagram on its surface, although other symbols may be depicted instead. As a magical implement the pentacle symbolizes the occultist's power to effect change in the physical realm. Taking this down a notch, in a nuts and bolts sense pentacles relate to our innate ability to make our way in the world and handle physical existence. They represent the survival stage of human development: the ability to find food and shelter and to reproduce successfully.

Next we look at the second part of the equation—the four levels of royalty.

ROYAL HIERARCHY AS STAGES OF CREATION

The Qabalah, as it is used in the Western Mysteries, grew out of the esoteric mystical branch of Judaism known as the Kabbalah. Both systems use the Tree of Life to describe divinity, existence, and humanity's purpose on earth. Simply stated, the Tree of Life consists of twenty-two paths that connect ten Sephiroth or spheres that express progressively denser stages of creation. Kether (Crown) is the topmost Sephirah and can be equated with divinity or Spirit. Malkuth (Kingdom) is the lowest and symbolizes the physical universe.

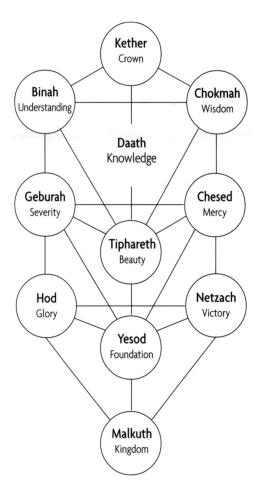

The Tree of Life: 10 Sephiroth and 22 Paths

On a more personal level each Sephirah can also be seen as an objective state of consciousness. The paths connecting any two Sephiroth describe the nature of the experience as one seeks to move from one state of consciousness (Sephirah) to another. So for example, the path connecting Malkuth and Yesod would describe the subjective experience of moving from sensate awareness of our physical mundane existence (Malkuth) to a state of heightened perceptivity (Yesod) where we behold perhaps the deeper meaning behind our existence.

Some argue that the Tarot emerged as a pictorial and symbolic representation of the Tree of Life. Indeed, the similarities between the twenty-two paths on the Tree and the twenty-two major arcana of the Tarot are informative and can contribute to the understanding of each. A little farther on I use the four Qabalistic worlds to clarify the four court card levels: king, queen, knight, and page.

The Qabalah teaches that manifested existence emerged in four stages. These four stages of creation, or the four worlds, as they are also known, evolved in the following order: Atziluth, Briah, Yetzirah, and Assiah. The four worlds correspond with the four letters of the

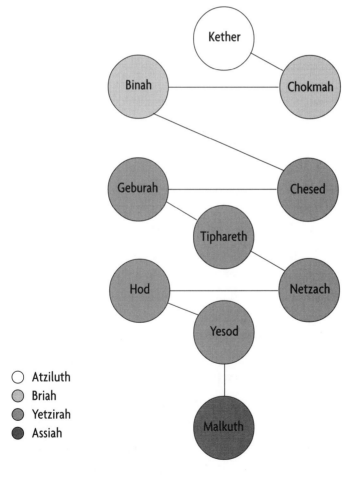

The Four Worlds on the Tree of Life and the Path of the Lightning Flash

tetragrammaton (Yod Heh Vau Heh) and can be superimposed upon the tree to show how manifestation flowed from Kether to Malkuth (known as "the path of the lightning flash").

Qabalists use varying systems to assign the worlds to the court card levels. I use the Golden Dawn system that places the kings in Atziluth, the queens in Briah, the knights/princes in Yetzirah, and the pages/princesses in Assiah.[2]

Kings: Atziluth—the Archetypal World

Spirit, impetus, the divine spark as our pure spiritual state, abstract concepts, divine consciousness, and the wellspring of creative force typify Atziluth. Atziluth is the world of ideas and inspiration and consists of the Sephirah Kether. This stage of creation relates to kings.

Queens: Briah—the Creative World

In the creative world of Briah, the idea or abstract concept develops into a latent, emerging form, rather like a sketch or mental image of what will be manifested in the final active world of Assiah. This stage of creation relates to queens. This is also the realm of the archangels.

Knights: Yetzirah—the Formative World

Yetzirah is the blueprint level of creation. The archetypal construct takes on detail and moves closer to its ultimate manifested form. Energy, thought, and emotion begin to specify the structure into a nearly operative prototype. This stage of creation relates to knights. This is also the realm of angels.

Pages: Assiah—the Active World

The formation of manifested existence as we know it in our everyday lives (i.e., earth, star, table, and animal) flows through four worlds transforming from idea to archetype to blueprint to manifested matter. Assiah is the world of physicality, substance, and completion. This stage of creation relates to pages.

COURT CARD FACES REVEALED

In the support-based approach, each suit represents an arena of life described by the key words spirit, love, knowledge, and power. When we combine these four concepts with the Qabalistic stages, represented by the king, queen, knight, and page, we can arrive at a systematic understanding of the role of each court card.

THE WAND COURT: SPIRIT
Supporters in the Spiritual Arena

KING OF WANDS
Spirit in the Archetypal World
Spiritual Elder
Spirit in the pure Atziluthic world of kings equates with the concept of enlightenment. As a supporter this becomes a Spiritual Elder, someone with otherworldly knowledge.

QUEEN OF WANDS
Spirit in the Creative World
Seer
In the Briatic world spiritual wisdom takes the form of the Seer who is able to perceive the latent archetypal forms that are emerging but not yet manifested such as future events or aspects of the Self.

KNIGHT OF WANDS
Spirit in the Formative World
Light Bringer
Now spiritual wisdom takes on more direction and structure. Creativity and humor come forth with the Light Bringer.

PAGE OF WANDS
Spirit in the Active World
Child
The pages of all suits indicate both beginning and ending. It is the final manifestation of what began in the Atziluthic world, but it is also the birth of a new form. One might say that a page is the king but on a different level, or that the page represents the spiritual ideal manifested in physical form—the Atziluthic spark manifesting in Assiah.

When we apply this concept to the Page of Wands, we see spirit manifested in physical form as a Child. Spiritual teachings often hold the child's mind—playful, authentic, spontaneous—as the mind-set adults should strive for when seeking enlightenment.

THE CUP COURT: LOVE
Supporters in the Emotional Arena

KING OF CUPS
Love in the Archetypal World
Benefactor
Love in its pure state is unconditional. The Benefactor expects nothing in return for his or her depth of acceptance.

QUEEN OF CUPS
Love in the Creative World
Confidante
In the Creative World, the Benefactor becomes more directed and personalized. The Confidante receives us with compassion and empathy while speaking from the truthful heart.

KNIGHT OF CUPS
Love in the Formative World
Lover
When love takes form and structure, it personifies as the Lover, someone who gives form to our hopes, feelings, or desires.

PAGE OF CUPS
Love in the Active World
Idol

Beauty might be described as the final physical expression of Atziluthic love. In other words, if love were to manifest in physical form, it would likely be a vision of beauty. An Idol is often a person whom we adore for his or her inner or outer beauty.

THE SWORD COURT: KNOWLEDGE
Supporters in the Mental Arena

KING OF SWORDS
Knowledge in the Archetypal World
Adviser

Knowledge in its pure state is the Adviser, someone we can turn to for advice because of his or her wide-ranging and in-depth knowledge. The Adviser accesses the mental world with ease.

QUEEN OF SWORDS
Knowledge in the Creative World
Exactor

When the Adviser enters into the more restrictive Briatic world, the Exactor manifests. This is someone who takes a more structured mental approach and may be someone in our lives who holds us to our promises, hones our thought processes, or points out our foibles.

KNIGHT OF SWORDS
Knowledge in the Formative World
Champion
Knowledge as it takes form and energy in the Yetziratic world can manifest as a Champion or someone who upholds or defends our cause and brings insight when we need it most.

PAGE OF SWORDS
Knowledge in the Active World
Student
In the physical world of Assiah the Student becomes the active seeker of knowledge and truth. Mental curiosity leads to intellectual growth and humankind's growing understanding of the universe.

THE PENTACLE COURT: POWER
Supporters in the Physical Arena

KING OF PENTACLES
Power in the Archetypal World
Mentor
Power manifesting in its pure Atziluthic state indicates physical mastery or mastery of a skill. *Mentor* describes the master whose gifts can now flow to others in the form of teaching.

QUEEN OF PENTACLES
Power in the Creative World
Healer
Here the mastery of the physical realm is applied on an energetic level. Power manifests as the Healer. Healing has to do with changing the physical structure of a body, but the changes first occur on an energetic level.

KNIGHT OF PENTACLES
Power in the Formative World
Protector
The Knight of Pentacles represents power manifesting in a more solid form. We turn to the Protector for physical stability and security.

PAGE OF PENTACLES
Power in the Active World
Apprentice
In a sense we all begin as an Apprentice in the world of Assiah learning the skills of life. More specifically we train Apprentice supporters in a trade or craft so they may carry on work we have begun and continue the progression of civilization.

The sixteen positions that I have briefly introduced above form the basis for

- Understanding the roles others play in our lives: supporters
- Recognizing unsupportive behavior in others: detractors
- Discovering our inner strengths: resources
- Recognizing limiting behavior in ourselves: challenges

Following are thumbnail sketches of the court card roles in each of the four modes: supporter, detractor, resource, and challenge.

COURT CARDS AS SUPPORTERS

Supporters are people in our lives who are special allies. They facilitate our growth in positive ways. Often supporters compensate for something we lack or are unable to see within ourselves. They fill a void we cannot yet fill for ourselves. They may also give us an extra push of energy, enabling us to accomplish a task, overcome a challenge, or have deeper insight. They root for us, lend an ear, or hold us to our promises.

COURT CARDS AS SUPPORTERS

Court Card	Wands (Spirit)	Cups (Love)	Swords (Knowledge)	Pentacles (Power)
King (Primal)	Spiritual Elder	Benefactor	Adviser	Mentor
Queen (Emergence)	Seer	Confidante	Exactor	Healer
Knight (Stabilization)	Light Bringer	Lover	Champion	Protector
Page (Completion)	Child	Idol	Student	Apprentice

COURT CARDS AS DETRACTORS

Each court card also has a negative side or obscured face. This is the reverse side of the positive supporter, which I have termed a detractor. Detractors present obstacles rather than support. However, in a deeper sense they can still be considered allies, for they challenge us to discover new strength within ourselves or push us to develop additional inner and outer resources. They often evoke and demand the best in our character.

COURT CARDS AS DETRACTORS

Court Card	Wands (Spirit)	Cups (Love)	Swords (Knowledge)	Pentacles (Power)
King (Primal)	Zealot	Betrayer	Dictator	Miser
Queen (Emergence)	Pretender	Victim	Critic	Abuser
Knight (Stabilization)	Trickster	Possessor	Rival	Deserter
Page (Completion)	Puer	Narcissist	Dabbler	Idler

COURT CARDS AS RESOURCES

Resources are like supporters except that rather than being external, they are parts of ourselves (knowledge, gifts, or skills) that lend us support or guide and aid us. These inner allies are sometimes called subpersonalities, inner figures, or archetypes. However we wish to name them, they are aspects of ourselves.

Inner allies are useful when we need to make it over a hurdle and outside support is unavailable. For example, if we do not have a Seer in our lives, then we may need to rely on our innate Self-Knowledge and inner vision by stretching our perceptivity. In a reading the Tarot court cards can sometimes point to hidden assets, abilities, or strengths of which we are unaware.

COURT CARDS AS RESOURCES

Court Card	Wands (Spirit)	Cups (Love)	Swords (Knowledge)	Pentacles (Power)
King (Primal)	Spiritual Vision	Unconditional Love	Pragmatism	Generosity
Queen (Emergence)	Self-Knowledge	Compassion	Discrimination	Self-Care
Knight (Stabilization)	Creativity	Desire	Insight	Trust
Page (Completion)	Play	Harmony	Curiosity	Diligence

COURTS CARDS AS CHALLENGES

Challenges represent "negative" character aspects that may need to be acknowledged, accepted, and transformed. They are the inner equivalent of the detractor. While not an exact match, a "challenge" can be likened to the Jungian concept of the shadow in the sense that these are parts of our personality that we are often unaware of and that perhaps are not within our conscious control.*

Challenges are unsupportive in the sense that they hinder and retard our growth or perception but supportive in the sense that they point to the areas where we need to grow and change. Psychologically they are all rooted in some kind of fear or misperception.

COURT CARDS AS CHALLENGES

Court Card	Wands (Spirit)	Cups (Love)	Swords (Knowledge)	Pentacles (Power)
King (Primal)	Illusion	Hatred	Ruthlessness	Greed
Queen (Emergent)	Self-Deception	Depression	Self-Criticism	Self-Destruction
Knight (Stabilization)	Boredom	Rejection	Anger	Neglect
Page (Completion)	Immaturity	Jealousy	Confusion	Inertia

IDENTIFY YOUR SUPPORTERS AND DETRACTORS

As you become familiar with the court cards and their roles, you will be able to quickly notice how people in your life support you and you them. Likewise, detractors will be readily apparent. You can use the following tables to begin to identify your supporters and detractors.

---

* As used in this book, *shadow* refers to a court card's baser, negative, or more undeveloped qualities of expression.

IDENTIFY YOUR SUPPORTERS

Name	Spiritual Elder	Seer	Light Bringer	Child	Benefactor	Confidante	Lover	Idol	Adviser	Exactor	Champion	Student	Mentor	Healer	Protector	Apprentice

IDENTIFY YOUR DETRACTORS

Name	Zealot	Pretender	Trickster	Puer	Betrayer	Victim	Possessor	Narcissist	Dictator	Critic	Rival	Dabbler	Miser	Abuser	Deserter	Idler

The next four chapters present the court cards in detail. The final four chapters demonstrate how to access the court card energies using divination, meditations, and pathworking.

KING of WANDS

QUEEN of WANDS.

KNIGHT of WANDS.

PAGE of WANDS.

FIVE
The Wand Court in the Kingdom of Spirit

The key words for the wand suit are *spirit, intuition, inspiration, wisdom, vision, creativity,* and *perception.* Wand supporters connect us with the spiritual level of our existence and our ability to conceive and implement creative ideas. They enlighten us by facilitating changes in our perception and lighten us through humor or play. Wand detractors create illusion and demonstrate how our ego can manipulate our sense of reality.

KING OF WANDS

Supporter: Spiritual Elder
Detractor: Zealot
Resource: Spiritual Vision
Challenge: Illusion

Supporter: Spiritual Elder

A Spiritual Elder is a spiritual teacher, sage, guru, shaman, magus, visionary, guide, the all-wise one. This is someone who provides illumination or shines light on a situation with spiritual knowledge.

*King of Staffs,
Alchemical Tarot*

*Chief of Pipes, Native
American Tarot*

He or she has intuitive understanding or direct knowledge of the workings of the spiritual worlds. Through teaching or presence the Spiritual Elder gives us a wider perspective, a sense of vision and spiritual inspiration. This person may be unassuming but with rare insight or may not even be incarnated. For example, Buddha, Yogananda, the Virgin of Guadalupe, or Christ may be a Spiritual Elder. The Spiritual Elder instills in us a sense of confidence about our place in the universal scheme of things.

Detractor: Zealot

In the extreme the Zealot can be a cult leader who has become enamored of sex, money, or power and abuses his or her position of authority. Or the Zealot can simply be someone who imposes his or her spiritual viewpoint upon others. The Zealot's spiritual vision is narrow, limiting, and exclusive. Having this detractor in our lives can cause us to lose confidence in our own ability to perceive spiritual truths and can sidetrack us from further spiritual growth. The Zealot challenges us to reconnect with our own version of spirituality and, on the other side of the coin, can be used as an opportunity to ask how we may be imposing our truths on others.

Resource: Spiritual Vision

Spiritual Vision describes our ability to perceive realities beyond our physical senses. This can include the ability to see auras and nonphysical beings or be receptive to communications from other realms via clairaudience, clairsentience, or clairvoyance. This capacity enables us to understand existence in the context of a greater plan. Sometimes this resource can be accessed through meditation, being in nature, or participating in a creative process such as music, writing, or art. I know one person who finds that high altitude (flying in an airplane or being in the mountains) activates his Spiritual Vision.

Challenge: Illusion

Spiritual Illusion may manifest as a fantasy regarding our spiritual mission or evolutionary status. In the extreme it may involve delusions such as believing we are the incarnated Christ, that we have attained the esoteric initiatory grade of Ipsissimus, or that we can save the world. These examples fall more within the realm of a psychological disorder; however, they demonstrate the type of Illusion the King of Wands can represent. The challenge is to pierce through the veil of illusion, maya, and ego inflation to come to a realistic understanding and acceptance of our role amid the mundane workings of existence.

King of Wands,
Spiral Tarot

Divination Guideline

If the King of Wands shows up in a reading, ask yourself:

- ♣ Who in my life enlightens me with spiritual knowledge or insight?

- ♣ How might this person help me in the given situation?

- ♣ Is there someone in my life who appears to be limiting my spiritual growth by imposing his or her spiritual truths or rules?

- ♣ Do I need to reassess my spiritual direction or commitments?

In a reading, the Spiritual Elder can also suggest

- ♣ An invitation to a vision quest

- ♣ A period of inner spiritual seeking

- ♣ The need for spiritual advice to gain a more expanded view of the situation at hand

- ♣ The ability to perceive nonphysical spiritual realities

- ♣ The influence of a spirit guide

- ♣ A tendency toward spiritual egotism

- ♣ The possibility of an unrealistic view of reality

The following vignette is an example of "Stepping into a Court Card," a meditation method described in chapter 11 that can be used with each of the sixteen court cards.

The King of Wands Speaks

It is warm. A lizard basks in the baking sun. Fire is expressed in the green growth of the wand. The fiery rays of the sun transform themselves into new growth, photosynthesis. I am the fire that seeds new growth: procreative, primitive, instinctive force. I travel the green halls of Victory where Venus rules.

My emblem is the ouroboros—the serpent that bites its own tail. I am the beginning and the end. I am the unchanging, universal law that "moves through all things." All beings begin their journey in my home, the glory of enlightenment, and return to me in the end. I am the vision of the whole. I am enlightenment through silence. My other emblem is the lion, whose red mane, like my own, boldly exclaims fiery passion. The lizard as my companion holds the prehistoric knowledge of humanity's beginnings and endings—cold-blooded, instinctive intelligence reminiscent of other environments, other existences, perhaps other planets.

In my negative aspect my fire voraciously consumes unabated. The cycle of transformation is turned in upon itself, eventually self-destructing in a demonical fiery blaze. The procreative forces of nature are directed into building power—a larger fire, a bigger blaze, more and more. The green vision of Venus no longer compels. My fire circumvented, redirected, feeds a growing illusion of grandeur.

♣

Wisdom is my name, flames crown my head, ever moving, ever dancing, never still.

QUEEN OF WANDS

Supporter: Seer
Detractor: Pretender
Resource: Self-Knowledge
Challenge: Self-Deception

Supporter: Seer

In the previous section we saw how the King of Wands as Spiritual Elder holds the vision of existence. In contrast, the Queen of Wands as Seer holds the vision of the Self. This is someone who uses his or her self-awareness to help us toward self-knowledge. The Seer treads the inner path ahead of us. This supporter may be someone in our lives who knows us deeply and holds a mirror for us to see our reflection. He or she may also be a talented intuitive or psychic.

Detractor: Pretender

The Queen of Wands as the Pretender, consciously or unconsciously, acts from pretense and falsity. The Pretender may also be someone who takes advantage of his or her intuitive abilities to manipulate others for personal gain. We may go to this detractor for help and instead receive misinformation and projections. The Pretender blocks the path to self-knowledge. When we look too often outside ourselves for validation and confirmation, we may attract this sort of person in our lives. Instead of providing answers, the Pretender pushes us to look within

Königin der Stäbe
Queen of Rods

Queen of Rods, Tarot of the Northern Shadows

to find our own way forward. Other words that might describe this detractor include liar, soothsayer, deceiver, or charlatan.

Resource: Self-Knowledge

The Queen of Wands as Self-Knowledge reflects our consistent effort to discover what lies beneath the persona we present to the world. We use this resource to perceive our underlying motives, illusions, and core truths and to express our unvarnished inner essence. Often we need to use a reflecting mirror such as a journal, dream work, or artistic expression to access Self-Knowledge. This resource also speaks of our intuition and inner vision and the understanding of our sexual nature.

Priestess of Wands,
Motherpeace Tarot

Challenge: Self-Deception

Who are we pretending to be? Are we acting from a false self? Have we convinced ourselves we are someone we are not? What parts of ourselves are we unaware of? Self-Deception can also indicate egoism or grandiose notions of self. This differs from the King of Wands' challenge of Illusion, a challenge that revolves around spiritual egoism. Self-Deception points to more personal issues. Examples of this type include acting sweet when we are very

Queen of Wands,
Spiral Tarot

angry, or inflating our achievements or qualifications. Below Self-Deception lies low self-esteem. The Queen of Wands in this aspect challenges us to drop pretense, accept who we are, and present a truer image to the world.

Divination Guideline

If the Queen of Wands shows up in a reading, ask yourself:

- ♣ Who in my life helps me to know myself?

- ♣ How might this person help me in my given situation?

- ♣ Is there someone in my life who is pretending to be someone he or she is not?

- ♣ Am I relying too much on others to tell me who I am?

In a reading, the Seer can also suggest

- ♣ An invitation to help others search for self

- ♣ A period of inner searching and taking stock of who we are

- ♣ The need to set new priorities based on who we are now

- ♣ The ability to know self

- ♣ A tendency toward self-delusion

- ♣ The possibility of thinking I am someone I am not

The Queen of Wands Speaks

Stop. Before you cross my threshold, take notice of my familiar. Call me a witch or an intelligent domesticated feline. Take your pick. Sheba is as black as the night, like my realm, the inner darkness of the soul. I am the door between the worlds of light and dark. I have the powers of fiery vision.

My fire shines light where others have no sight. My crown grows leaves of inner wisdom. My emblem is the sunflower. Each seed of its fertile core is a flame of inner knowing and passion. These flames are the many eyes of the soul that follow the traveling light of the sun shining within. I am fertility of the soul. My inner knowing brings forth creative abundance.

In my darker aspect sunflowers wither and die. Their heavy heads hang bowed, with empty sockets staring blankly at the ground below, unaware of the beaming rays of the sun. My penetrating vision becomes distorted. I see half-truths, false hopes, and passing shadows.

♣

Call me Seer of inner light.

KNIGHT OF WANDS

Supporter: Light Bringer
Detractor: Trickster
Resource: Creativity
Challenge: Boredom

Supporter: Light Bringer

The Light Bringer is someone who brings lightness to our life through humor, inspiration, optimism, and creativity. It is probably no accident that the word *humor* was once related to health. Have you ever noticed how humor heals, or how much better you feel after a good laugh? This supporter also represents people in our life who heal us spiritually or lighten our moods. The Light Bringer introduces surprise, excitement, and unpredictability into our lives. He or she may be called the joker, or wild card. This person will have a tendency to see things differently, prod us to change our views, and ask us to lighten up. This supporter may enter our life only briefly, to pivotally alter our direction, and may be someone whose purpose is directed by an inner vision.

Detractor: Trickster

As a detractor, the Knight of Wands is a master of illusion. This is someone who avoids making promises and who slips away when we try to hold him or her accountable. In fact, when we do, we often find the tables turned and suddenly we

Son of Wands,
Motherpeace Tarot

are to blame! The Trickster is slippery, elusive, and manipulative. Ridicule and sarcasm may be part of this detractor's modus operandi. This person's version of the truth leaves us asking, "What is real here?" The Trickster challenges us to pierce a veil of illusion.

Prince of Wands, Thoth Tarot

Resource: Creativity

The resource for the Knight of Wands is Creativity—our capacity to have new ideas and follow through with their implementation. If you have ever been absorbed in a creative project, you know what this resource is about. Being in touch with Creativity increases our energy, gives us purpose, and can strengthen our ability to heal others and ourselves. This connection to emotional and spiritual healing is why creative expressions such as music, art, dance, and sexual play can bring balance, energy, and optimism back into our lives.

Challenge: Boredom

When we are frustrated, blocked, or without adequate creative outlets, we may end up feeling bored with our lives and impatient with those around us. Perhaps we need to wonder how our attitude, feelings, or physical energy might be limiting our ability to have fun, be creative, or enjoy our sexuality. The challenge is to find a source of inspiration and start a creative flow.

Divination Guideline

If the Knight of Wands shows up in a reading, ask yourself:

♣ Who in my life makes me laugh?

♣ How might this person help me in my given situation?

♣ Is there someone in my life who brings me down with sarcasm or ridicule?

♣ What is real here?

In a reading, the Light Bringer can also suggest

♣ An invitation to go on an adventure or start a creative project

♣ A period of inspired creativity

♣ The need for a sense of humor

♣ The ability to facilitate growth in others

♣ A tendency toward projection, sarcasm, or ridicule

♣ The possibility of being tricky or manipulating through falsity

The Knight of Wands Speaks

I spread like fire. I am contagious laughter—rippling, darting, dancing flames of merriment. I am confident, extroverted, and enthusiastic. I am a doer and on a mission to inspire awe, creativity, excitement, adventure, and daring. I am like fire in the desert—contained. My outer purpose is directed by an inner vision. I am inspired vision in action. I can be a leader and attract followers.

In my negative aspect my creative vision is not grounded in a sense of inner purpose. I have no real destination. I ride on my attractive steed in a barren desert going from oasis to oasis—from one illusion to another. I tell tall tales of great deeds to those who gather around me. The ancient pyramids of inner mystery erode into dunes of shifting grains of sand. I am a master of illusion. Many are fooled by me and join me in my traveling circus. I can be self-indulgent and superficial.

♣

I use humor to inspire and irony to help others take themselves less seriously.

PAGE OF WANDS

Supporter: Child
Detractor: Puer
Resource: Play
Challenge: Immaturity

Supporter: Child

As mentioned earlier, some spiritual traditions use the example of a child's mind-set to epitomize the state of enlightenment. It is true. Children frequently express profound truths in such simplicity that we shake our heads, wondering how a child could have expressed such wisdom. Children are sometimes our best teachers. Likewise the supporter Child can enlighten and inspire us with his or her idealism, youthful curiosity, and zest for life. This person does not have to be a child but might be described as youthful regardless of age. This might also be someone with whom we "play" and have fun.

Detractor: Puer

As a detractor the Page of Wands is the Puer. This is someone who for one reason or another refuses to grow up and accept the responsibilities of life. His or her irresponsible behavior can cause us to take on more than our share of responsibility. This detractor may in fact be well-meaning or be following a cherished ideal of how life *should* be lived. However, if we have a bit of the Puer in us as well, we can be seduced into his or her fantasy world. The Puer calls on us to take a look at our responsibilities and how we are fulfilling them. The

Bube der Stäbe
Page of Rods

Page of Rods,
Tarot of the
Northern Shadows

Page of Wands in this capacity may cause us to examine how we set limits with others and with ourselves.

Resource: Play

So, when was the last time you went out and played? Not enough time? Too much to do? Have other priorities? Do you remember how to play or know what brings you delight? Some of us are more serious than others, but we all have the inherent ability to play. Playing sports or games, working a jigsaw puzzle, reading a novel, going to the movies, eating popcorn, coloring, baking cookies, and listening to music with friends are ways to access this resource. Play can bring inspiration into our lives. The Page of Wands in this capacity may also indicate the sexual excitement associated with adolescence.

Challenge: Immaturity

Immaturity, on the other hand, is about avoiding responsibility in order to have fun. It may also be about building castles in the air and wishful thinking. Or it can indicate a lack of worldly experience that affects our ability to make sound decisions. In all these cases, the "world of hard knocks" eventually brings about greater maturity and a new set of priorities.

Princess of Wands,
Spiral Tarot

This challenge may also present itself when we hold on to unrealistic hopes or desires around relationships, especially those with our parents. The challenge in this regard is to arrive at acceptance of what we did not receive in the relationship, and eventually move on.

Divination Guideline

If the Page of Wands shows up in a reading, ask yourself:

♣ Who in my life brings me out to play?

♣ How might this person help me in my given situation?

♣ Is there someone in my life who is being irresponsible or childish?

♣ How am I contributing to or supporting his or her destructive behavior?

In a reading, the Child can also suggest

♣ An invitation to play

♣ A period of fun, spontaneity, experimentation

♣ The need for a new or youthful outlook

♣ The ability to communicate simple but profound truths

♣ A tendency toward unrealistic expectations and rebellion

♣ The possibility of holding on to a childhood fantasy

The Page of Wands Speaks

Do not let appearances fool you. I am the eternal child whose innocent giggles of delight echo in your soul. I gaze at my wand as I do at each new discovery—with fascination and intent. I am curiosity and wonder. I like to play and have fun and build idyllic imaginary worlds where I can roam. My fantasies can be idealistic but touch the inner hopes and dreams shared by many. I believe in fairies. I am naïve and new. I am easily bruised; treat me gently. My vision is your lifeblood; take me away and watch your desire wither and die.

In my negative aspect I lose myself in fantasy. Or I get angry that my fantasies are not real and become delinquent, destructive, and irresponsible. The harsh realities of life mar my youthful vision. I become despondent and feel deeply disappointed. There is no good in the world. There is no place for me. I do what I can to escape the unpleasantness of my life. I vent my frustration through destructive behavior.

♣

Let me wander through your life, free spirited and unshackled.

The following table presents a range of interpretations traditionally assigned to the wand court cards. Similar tables pertaining to the other suits appear at the end of chapters 6 through 8. The tables are organized thematically and derived from a variety of sources that are listed below each. The charts can be used as a quick reference guide and point to other sources that could be helpful with regard to court card interpretation.

WAND COURT CARDS: A RANGE OF DIVINATORY MEANINGS AND ASSOCIATIONS

Court Card	King	Queen	Knight	Page
Historical Person	Alexander	Argine	None	Lancelot
Grimaud	Spiritual force brings	Fatality, defense by means of mediation in discussions,	Providential aid, support brutality, passionate anger	Hard work with chance of success given in everything moral support
Character	Family man, swift, strong, hasty, violent, just, generous, noble, agile, virile, passionate, traditional, loyal	Gossip, flirt, social, practical	Friendly, active, generous, fierce, impetuous, prideful, impulsive, unpredictable, bigoted	Courage, brilliance, daring, vigor, energy, impression of beauty, enthusiastic
Appearance	Blond hair, blue or hazel eyes, mature man	Blond hair, blue or hazel eyes, mature woman	Blond hair, blue or hazel eyes, young man	Boy or girl with blond hair, blue or hazel eyes
Occupation	Manager, grand master, notary, clergyman, country gentleman	Head of established institutions, country woman, counselor, mother	Occultist, traveler	Postman, envoy, brother, schoolmate
Psychic	Deliberation, advice should be followed	Fertility, money matters, goodwill	Change of residence, departure, migration, travel, separation	Messages of love or hope, helpful influences
Elemental	Fire of Fire	Water of Fire	Air of Fire	Earth of Fire
Qabalistic	Chokmah in Atziluth	Binah in Atziluth	Tiphareth in Atziluth	Malkuth in Atziluth

WAND COURT CARDS: A RANGE OF DIVINATORY MEANINGS AND ASSOCIATIONS (continued)

Court Card	King	Queen	Knight	Page
Astrology	20° Scorpio to 20° Sagittarius; Nov. 13–Dec. 12	20° Pisces to 20° Aries; March 11–April 10	20° Cancer to 20° Leo; July 12–Aug. 11	June 21–Sept. 22
I Ching Hexagram	51: *Chên*, the Arousing	17: *Sui*, Following	42: *I*, Increase	27: *I*, the Corners of the Mouth
Tattwa	Red triangle in red triangle	Silver crescent in red triangle	Blue circle in red triangle	Yellow square in red triangle
Psychology	*Arrien:* Changes our perception of the world, committed to spiritual growth *Greer:* Establishment of self, ability to be oneself, achievement oriented	*Arrien:* Knower of self. Desires more self-knowledge *Greer:* Recognizes personal power, displays self-confidence, generosity	*Arrien:* Spiritual creativity manifested in the world *Greer:* Putting energy into self-growth, future prospects, new directions, willing to take risks, inspired enthusiasm	*Arrien:* Spiritual evolution. Freedom from fear *Greer:* Seeks new directions for self-growth, daring, uninhibited
Support Role	Spiritual Elder	Seer	Light Bringer	Child

Sources

Historical person: *The Encyclopedia of Tarot*, Stuart R. Kaplan. Grimaud: *The Dictionary of the Tarot*, Bill Butler. Character, occupation, psychic: compilation of various authors' interpretations as found in *Dictionary of the Tarot*, Butler.

Elemental: *The Golden Dawn*, Israel Regardie. Qabalistic: *Self-Initiation into the Golden Dawn Tradition*, Chic Cicero and Sandra Tabatha Cicero. Astrology: *The Book of Thoth*, Aleister Crowley. I Ching Hexagram: *Book of Thoth*, Crowley; *The I Ching*, trans. by Richard Wilhelm and Cary F. Baynes. Tattwa: *Tattwa: Tarot Mirrors*, Mary K. Greer. Appearance: *A Complete Guide to the Tarot*, Eden Gray. Psychology: *The Tarot Handbook*, Angeles Arrien; *Tarot for Your Self*, Mary K. Greer.

KING of CUPS.

QUEEN of CUPS.

KNIGHT of CUPS.

PAGE of CUPS.

SIX

The Cup Court in the Kingdom of Love

The key words for the cup suit are *love, emotion, relationship, hope, inspiration,* and *the unconscious.* Cup supporters influence and nurture the feeling level of our existence. By raising difficult emotional hurdles, cup detractors indirectly challenge us to find new inner strength.

KING OF CUPS

Supporter: Benefactor
Detractor: Betrayer
Resource: Unconditional Love
Challenge: Hatred

Supporter: Benefactor

The Benefactor sits upon the grail throne as the font of goodwill and inexhaustible love. The King of Cups is someone in our life who loves us unconditionally. We can rely on the Benefactor to love us no matter what we do or say. He or she may get angry at us and even at times dislike who

*Roi de Coupe, Oswald
Wirth Tarot*

we are, yet the Benefactor's love for us is unfailing. Grandparents, parents, or offspring can act as Benefactors. Another permutation may be a counselor or therapist who shows unconditional positive regard and accepts us "as is."

Like the King of Wands Spiritual Elder, the Benefactor does not have to be someone who is incarnated. We may feel this sort of unconditional acceptance from a special god or goddess, a savior-type spiritual figure, or even ancestors we have never met. This is love that has no boundaries. Mother Teresa acted as a Benefactor for many people.

Detractor: Betrayer

The King of Cups as a detractor is the Betrayer. This is someone who violates our trust. He or she breaks an implied promise to remain true and loyal. Betrayal can take many forms; in the worst case betrayal can be devastating and greatly hamper our ability to function normally. We wonder if it was our fault, if it was something we did or said. We can end up blaming ourselves for something that may have been entirely out of our control. An example of this is the child who blames herself for her parents' divorce. The presence of this detractor calls on us to search within for self-acceptance.

*King of Vessels,
Alchemical Tarot*

Resource: Unconditional Love

As an inner resource the King of Cups represents our capacity for emotional openness. Unconditional Love speaks of our ability to accept others deeply despite their shortcomings and to love ourselves in the same way. The King of Cups in this mode may also refer to staying true to our commitments in the face of great difficulties. In addition, Unconditional Love may be a test of our ability to forgive those who have harmed or hurt us in some "unforgivable" way.

Challenge: Hatred

Experiences such as betrayal, abuse, ridicule, neglect, criticism, or rejection can lead to feelings of hatred. For example, when we feel betrayed, it is easy to hate the betrayer or even to hate ourselves, as evidenced in an act of accepting responsibility. Beneath the hatred is usually a deep hurt. Hatred paradoxically brings both intimacy and separation. Hatred is intimate in its very intensity, very similar to the way that love is intimate. However, hatred also brings a wall of separation, alienation, and noncommunication. The King of Cups as an inner challenge asks us to come to terms with the wound lying beneath the defensive veneer of loathing that may make us appear to others as cold, frigid, aloof, unkind, or disconnected.

Divination Guide

If the King of Cups shows up in a reading, ask yourself:

- ♥ Who in my life loves me unconditionally?

- ♥ How might this person help me in my given situation?

- ♥ Is there someone in my life who has betrayed me?

- ♥ Has this person's betrayal affected my self-esteem?

In a reading, the Benefactor can also suggest

- ♥ An invitation to be at peace with oneself

♥ A period of deep emotional connectedness with others

♥ The need for self-acceptance

♥ The ability to be loyal and committed to others

♥ A tendency toward lack of faith or distrust

♥ The possibility of having betrayed self or others

The King of Cups Speaks

I am stability within fluidity. The winsome song of the whale reverberates my love through the ocean depths, permeating everything within. My strength lies in the breadth of the ocean. I absorb all that is cast onto me, whether it be boulders or pebbles. Touch me and let the whale's song of love fill your soul.

In my negative aspect the ocean waters become treacherous and stormy and I betray those who have come to trust me. Darkness and hatred pollute my depths. I contaminate others with the sharp, lashing waves of my tongue and the coldness of my sterile womb.

♥

I am deep fathomless love that has no boundaries.

QUEEN OF CUPS

Supporter: Confidante
Detractor: Victim
Resource: Compassion
Challenge: Depression

Supporter: Confidante

The Queen of Cups is the Confidante and is the ideal of a true friend. This is someone who is empathic to our situation and shows us compassion. He or she listens to our outpourings and reflects back our experience in a way that clarifies and enables us to move on in our process. Yet the Confidante is not always "sweetness and light." He or she will also speak the truth. The Queen of Cups in this capacity has a knack for understanding what we are feeling maybe even better than we do.

XXXVIII. THE MISTRESS OF
THE CUP

The Mistress of the Cup,
Egyptian Tarot

Detractor: Victim

The Victim blames others for his or her own difficult life circumstance. Everyone else is at fault for the Victim's misfortune. This detractor may also be someone who offers compassion to the point of self-sacrifice. He or she is unable to set boundaries, giving all and more of what is asked. The end result, though, is that this person feels victimized and used. He or she may complain of being treated like a doormat but is unwilling to set limits with others to gain respect. The Queen of Cups as Victim may also revel in misfortune, encouraging both sympathy and more abuse

Queen of Cups,
Spiral Tarot

in order to perpetuate the cycle through manipulative behavior. The Victim's attention can be smothering. This detractor may cause us to take on a draining and perhaps unnecessary caretaking role. (As an aside, there are people who are truly victims either of a crime or of other difficult life circumstances. This category is not speaking of them. See Page of Pentacles, p. 125.)

Resource: Compassion

As a resource the Queen of Cups represents our ability to offer compassion to ourselves and to others. How does this differ from the King of Cups and Unconditional Love? Compassion is more specific, referring to individual circumstances and the ability to empathize and be emotionally honest. Compassion does not ask us to love unconditionally. We merely need to listen, understand, and communicate our understanding to those who are asking for our support. This is the ability to be empathic and access the power of the unconscious.

The Queen of Cups is about knowing the ebb and flow of our emotional tide and expressing this truth to others—the truthful heart.

Matriarch of Vessels,
Native American Tarot

Challenge: Depression

As a challenge the Queen of Cups represents feeling depressed, lost, or numb. Perhaps we have given too much of ourselves, been victimized or trampled, suffered a great loss, or have a broken heart. Many roads lead to depression, including our biochemistry, and volumes of books have been written on the topic. But for the "garden variety" depression that many of us experience, our challenge is to both identify and express our feelings (oftentimes anger) and find a way to place events in perspective so we can find our way back on track.

Divination Guide

If the Queen of Cups shows up in a reading, ask yourself:

- ♥ Who in my life is a true friend and is there with deep compassion when I need it?

- ♥ How might this person help me in my given situation?

- ♥ Is there someone in my life who is acting the victim?

- ♥ Is there a need for me to set boundaries, emotional or otherwise, with this person?

In a reading, the Confidante can also suggest

- ♥ An invitation to spend time with a close friend

- ♥ A period of getting in touch with deeper emotions

- ♥ The need to be honest with self and others about our feelings

- ♥ The ability to be compassionate

- ♥ A tendency toward feeling oneself to be a victim and not setting boundaries

- ♥ The possibility of feeling depressed

The Queen of Cups Speaks

My throne is on the shifting sands of the shore. Shells are my emblem, opening and closing to the rhythm of my heart. I know my tides and follow their rhythms. My love is contained yet steady, forming a reservoir of compassion for others to be soothed by.

In my negative aspect I become lost in the churning sea of emotion. Who am I? I feel powerless and victimized by the turbulent waters. I feel overwhelmed and see no way to help myself. I succumb and give myself to the mercy of others.

♥

I am the compassionate and loyal heart.

KNIGHT of CUPS.

KNIGHT OF CUPS

Supporter: Lover
Detractor: Possessor
Resource: Desire
Challenge: Rejection

Supporter: Lover

As a supporter the Knight of Cups is the Lover. The Lover inspires our passion for life. This may be someone we have fallen in love with or with whom we share a great passion. The Lover may also be a person in whose presence we feel a spark of attraction, admiration, and deep connection. The Knight of Cups as Lover makes us feel alive and vibrant.

Alternatively, the Knight of Cups might represent an abstract ideal or goal that holds a stirring excitement, for example, the desire to travel around the world or to climb Mount Everest or even to raise a family. In a reading the Knight of Cups may also be a secret admirer.

Detractor: Possessor

As a detractor the Knight of Cups is the Possessor. This is someone whose passion has become self-serving or possessive. His or her attachment to us can have an addicted, needy, or clinging quality. He or she may be in need of constant reassurance. The Possessor's desire for our attention is uncontained and we may feel trapped, overwhelmed, or smothered. This detractor challenges us to ask how our relationship needs are being met.

KNIGHT OF CUPS

Knight of Cups, Tarot of Marseilles

Ritter der Kelche
Knight of Cups

Knight of Cups, Tarot of the Northern Shadows

Resource: Desire

Desire can move mountains. It is an incredibly strong motivating force. As an inner resource the Knight of Cups relates to our capacity to access this emotional fuel to energize our lives through fantasy, dreams and the imagination. Desire may also relate to loving someone passionately or living our life with exuberance and joy. Our enthusiasm may inspire others.

Challenge: Rejection

As a challenge the Knight of Cups represents our tendency to reject someone or something we feel we cannot have or do not deserve. We may even reject what we most desire instead of confronting the fear that our desires may not be fulfilled or the pain if they are not. The Knight of Cups can also show up as the face of fickleness. We might be moody, unpredictable, undependable, or unfaithful. This challenge asks us to examine ways we reject ourselves and those around us. How is it easier for us to reject than to accept?

Divination Guide

If the Knight of Cups shows up in a reading, ask yourself:

♥ Who in my life inspires me to or is a model of great passion?

♥ How might this person help me in my given situation?

♥ Is there someone in my life who is needy or possessive?

♥ Is this relationship part of a larger pattern?

In a reading, the Lover can also suggest

♥ An invitation to a love tryst

♥ A time of great passion for someone or something

♥ The need for dreams, fantasies, or a secret interest

♥ The ability to be fueled by desire

♥ A tendency toward fickleness or inappropriate attachment

♥ The possibility of rejecting something or someone of value

The Knight of Cups Speaks

I am the winged messenger of love. Solomon is my king. I am visions, dreams, hopes, and desires. I often come at a crossroads where a leap of faith over an unknown depth must take place. I am inspiration and fantasy—mind in the heart. I offer an opportunity, an entanglement, a dance, an affair, a tryst with passion. I offer the Lover's cup for you to drink from.

In my negative aspect I am the Possessor. I offer a cup of brackish water, for my desire runs unabated. The drink I offer does not quench but holds others to me, imprisoned now by a growing thirst. What I cannot have I reject or seek to destroy.

♥

I am the potent force of desire.

PAGE OF CUPS

Supporter: Idol
Detractor: Narcissist
Resource: Harmony
Challenge: Jealousy

Supporter: Idol

The Page of Cups represents the concept of love in its most physical form, beauty. Beauty is a particular configuration of qualities that evokes inspiration. For example, when we are in the presence of beauty in nature, we are often accompanied by feelings of balance and tranquillity.

PAGE of CUPS.

Bube der Kelche
Page of Cups

Page of Cups,
Tarot of the
Northern Shadows

Likewise, when we are in the presence of the Idol, this supporter's inner or outer beauty can evoke feelings of peacefulness and harmony. We can also become inspired, come in touch with a sense of divine beauty, or even experience a heightened sense of life's perfection.

Detractor: Narcissist

As a detractor the Page of Cups is the Narcissist. This is a person who is preoccupied with looks and image. Inner beauty remains undiscovered. Around this detractor we feel inconsequential, less than, forgotten, or swallowed in his or her world. In extreme cases we lose a sense of ourselves and our personal identity. The challenge is to distinguish ourselves from this detractor and begin acting in the world from our own center of being.

Resource: Harmony

The resource of the Page of Cups is Harmony. Our emotions are in balance. We have neutrality and detachment and are emotionally secure. When our heart is in balance we can confidently reach out in new directions for relationships without fear of loss or hurt. We can approach people with trust, innocence, and openness. The Page of Cups

Daughter of Cups,
Motherpeace Tarot

also relates to our ability to heal and recover from emotional wounds. The resource of Harmony speaks of our ability to rejuvenate, regenerate, and maintain an open heart.

Challenge: Jealousy

"Mirror, mirror, here I stand, who is the fairest in the land?"[1] Snow White's stepmother exemplifies both the detractor and the challenge of the Page of Cups. She was preoccupied with her looks (Narcissist) and sent Snow White to meet her doom because she deplored having anyone near who might be more beautiful (Jealousy). To be perfectly fair to stepmom, she probably had a father or mother who was overly critical of her (Queen of Swords Critic), hence her lack of self-esteem. Characteristics of Jealousy are selfishness, narcissism, and insecurity.

Divination Guideline

If the Page of Cups shows up in a reading, ask yourself:

♥ Who in my life inspires me by his or her presence or beauty?

♥ How might this person help me in my given situation?

♥ Is there someone in my life who thinks only of him- or herself and ignores me?

♥ How can I make room for myself in this relationship?

In a reading, the Idol can also suggest

♥ An invitation to a new relationship

♥ A period devoted to inner and outer beauty

♥ The need for harmony and inner balance

♥ The ability to heal emotionally

♥ A tendency toward narcissism or selfishness

♥ The possibility of feeling jealous

The Page of Cups Speaks

I am the lively personification of love. Seaweed is my princely crown. I stand upon a pier, center stage. I have little to my name. I am ephemeral—of this world but not. In my cup is the fish that adorns the king. I stare at the harvest of the sea as if I stare at a reflection of myself. For it is I. I am the worldly reflection of the watery realm of love and beauty. My outer beauty reflects an inner balance, a tranquility and acceptance of what is. My heart is open to new experience and without worries or sorrow.

In my negative aspect, I become absorbed with my position onstage, and the ocean mirror lures me like an obsession. I do nothing but peer at my beautiful reflection, oblivious to my surroundings—in love with what I see and unable to see anything else. I become snagged like a fish upon a barbed hook, and my heart closes.

Nothing must interrupt my afflicted attention. The reflection must be in love with me. If it dares to form a life of its own and let its eyes wander from my grasping gaze, then I become the jealous heart.

♥

I am harmony.

CUP COURT CARDS: A RANGE OF DIVINATORY MEANINGS AND ASSOCIATIONS

Court Card	King	Queen	Knight	Page
Historical Person	Charlemagne	Judith	None	la Hire
Grimaud	Knowledge and abundance, possessions safeguarded and protected	Wisdom prevails, good advice	None	Spiritual and moral riches obtained as a reward
Character	Kind, big spender, sensitive, subtle, intensely secret, fair, calm exterior, violent, idealistic	Good, fair, honest, devoted, does service, loving, intelligent, gift of vision, friend, imaginative, poetic	Fair, Venusian, dreamer, sensitive, sensual, passive, graceful	Fair, studious, gracious, sweet, voluptuous, imaginative, dreamy
Occupation	Tutor, teacher, artist, doctor, hunter, philosopher	Poet, wife, mother, mistress, barmaid	Lover, seducer, teacher, sailor	Bachelor
Psychic	Scandal, hope and promise, traveling by sea	Success, pleasure, happiness, promotion, fame	Fraud, drugs	Coming of messages, birth, news, proposal of marriage
Elemental	Fire of Water	Water of Water	Air of Water	Earth of Water
Qabalistic	Chokmah in Briah	Binah in Briah	Tiphareth in Briah	Malkuth in Briah
Astrology	20° Aquarius to 20° Pisces; Feb. 9–March 10	20° Gemini to 20° Cancer; June 11–July 11	20° Libra to 20° Scorpio; Oct. 13–Nov. 12	Sept. 23–Dec. 21

CUP COURT CARDS: A RANGE OF DIVINATORY MEANINGS AND ASSOCIATIONS (continued)

Court Card	King	Queen	Knight	Page
I Ching Hexagram	54: *Kuei Mei,* the Marrying Maiden	58: *Tui;* the Joyous, Lake	61: *Chung Fu,* Inner Truth	41: *Sun,* Decrease
Tattwa	Red triangle in silver crescent	Silver crescent in silver crescent	Blue circle in silver crescent	Yellow square in silver crescent
Appearance	Light brown hair, hazel eyes, mature man	Light brown hair, hazel eyes, mature woman	Light brown hair, hazel eyes, young man	Boy or girl with light brown hair, hazel eyes
Psychology	*Arrien:* The optimist, openly loving, giving totally, loyal *Greer:* Established emotions or relationship, ability to love, counselor	*Arrien:* Emotional reflector, commitment to be true to the Self, reflects feelings accurately *Greer:* Channels feelings and emotions, dreams, visions, psychic	*Arrien:* The lover, emotional, passion, desire *Greer:* Following your dreams, visions, ideals, love	*Arrien:* Emotional detachment, free of jealousy, emotional longevity *Greer:* Open to love and new relationships, willing to take risks with love
Support Role	Benefactor	Confidante	Lover	Idol

Sources

Historical person: *The Encyclopedia of Tarot,* Stuart R. Kaplan. Grimaud: *The Dictionary of the Tarot,* Bill Butler.

Character, occupation, psychic: compilation of various authors' interpretations as found in *Dictionary of the Tarot,* Bill Butler. Elemental: *The Golden Dawn,* Israel Regardie. Qabalistic: *Self-Initiation into the Golden Dawn Tradition,* Chic Cicero and Sandra Tabatha Cicero. Astrology: *The Book of Thoth,* Aleister Crowley. I Ching Hexagram: *Book of Thoth,* Crowley; *The I Ching,* trans. by Richard Wilhelm and Cary F. Baynes. Tattwa: *Tarot Mirrors,* Mary K. Greer. Appearance: *A Complete Guide to the Tarot,* Eden Gray. Psychology: *The Tarot Handbook,* Angeles Arrien; *Tarot for Your Self,* Mary K. Greer.

KING of SWORDS.

QUEEN of SWORDS.

KNIGHT of SWORDS.

PAGE of SWORDS.

SEVEN

The Sword Court in the Kingdom of Knowledge

The key words for the sword suit are *knowledge, intellect, logic, reason, mind, morals, attitude,* and *truth.* Sword supporters have to do with the mental level of our existence. They help us to clarify our thinking and organize our actions. Sword detractors tend to pursue conflict and confrontation and can also exhibit mental rigidity or confusion. Sword detractors reflect how our minds create inner and outer conflict.

KING OF SWORDS

Supporter: Adviser
Detractor: Dictator
Resource: Pragmatism
Challenge: Ruthlessness

Supporter: Adviser

Archetypally, this supporter is the wise adviser to the king. The Adviser represents mastery of the intellect and worldly knowledge. The King of Swords may be insightful about morals or law. He or she holds

KING of SWORDS.

95

König der Schwerter
King of Swords

King of Swords, Tarot of the Northern Shadows

the "big picture." The Adviser has answers to a wide variety of questions and has a conceptual understanding of the world that makes this supporter the ideal resource when we need to figure out our options. The King of Swords can be someone with wide-ranging life experience or someone who is naturally pragmatic and clear thinking. Occasionally a child will have this gift, the ability to understand complicated situations conceptually and distill issues and options. An Adviser may also be someone who has specialized knowledge. Seek out an Adviser to analyze and clarify.

Detractor: Dictator

The King of Swords as a detractor may have excellent analytical skills but leaves out the human element when considering options. The Dictator may appear heartless but well equipped with a cold and calculating mind. He or she makes decisions based upon the bottom line, disregarding emotional repercussions the decision might have. Numerous political leaders, past and present, typify this type of tyrannical or autocratic detractor. On a more personal level, this may be someone who tries to dictate how we act, think, or feel, causing us to feel trapped, afraid, or emotionally shut down. The Dictator calls on us to find our truth and stand by it.

KING OF SWORDS

King of Swords, Alchemical Tarot

Resource: Pragmatism

As an inner resource the King of Swords represents pragmatism, or our ability to analyze situations and proceed with what works. Our actions are practical and applied in a no-frills approach to getting things done. This resource can also represent our ability to focus, concentrate, and be mentally determined.

Use this inner ally to set and achieve goals and to move forward when the going gets rough or motivation wanes.

A word can also be said here for another side to this resource: the tranquil mind. Great clarity of thinking can arise from the fertile ground of stillness.

Challenge: Ruthlessness

King of Swords,
Spiral Tarot

The King of Swords as an inner challenge is Ruthlessness. This is the Dictator turned inward. When we are in this mode we wield the sword to cut away hopes and feelings. We deem them impractical, childish, or far-fetched. We might take this approach to reach a desired goal, or we might have taken on this sort of self-denial as a way of being. However, when we sell out our dreams and refuse to acknowledge our emotions, we deny a part of ourselves. This challenge, even in a mild form, can affect our relationships. Others may not feel completely heard or accepted around our cut-and-dried approach. This is the ruthless mind in action.

Divination Guideline

If the King of Swords shows up in a reading, ask yourself:

♠ Who in my life can I count on for practical advice or knowledge?

♠ How might this person help me in my given situation?

♠ Is there someone in my life who is dictating how I think or act?

♠ Am I selling out for some goal that is not worth the price?

In a reading, the Adviser can also suggest

♠ An invitation to share knowledge gained

♠ A period of directed thinking, incoming information

♠ The need for practical, pragmatic advice

♠ The ability to analyze

♠ A tendency toward intellectual control and discounting emotions

♠ The possibility of not taking into account your or others' feelings

The King of Swords Speaks

A light cool breeze blows atop the pine-covered knoll. Behind the knoll, far below lies the ocean. Birds gaily sing, unbothered by the frozen royal figure sitting upon the throne. Suddenly he smiles. His sharp blue eyes come to life, and the eerie, piercing stare of the ice king melts. He speaks:

I am the penetrating mind. I am rationality and logic. I am the accumulation of fact and the application thereof. I am order. I am truth. I am the mind that distills right from wrong. I am morality. I am the basis of civilization. I am knowledge, intelligence, golden light. I am the clear and perceptive communicating mind. I am that which you are using right now. I make you human and take you above the instinctive animal nature of the creature kingdom. I magically transform the earthbound caterpillar into the graceful, ethereal butterfly. I communicate with angels and humans; I am the trained and untrained mind. The sword as my emblem represents defense, strategy, duality, and reality. It cuts and severs in two.

In my negative aspect I become locked in a single mode. I am unable to use the flexibility of the mind to see alternatives and perceive duality. I become ruthless in the pursuit of a single goal or direction. No other reasoning or logic makes any sense to me. I am right; all other ways are wrong.

♠

Call me the lucid thinker.

QUEEN OF SWORDS

Supporter: Exactor
Detractor: Critic
Resource: Discrimination
Challenge: Self-Criticism

Supporter: Exactor

The Queen of Swords supports us in the role of Exactor. This is the person in our life we can rely on to set us right in no uncertain terms. He or she will "call us on our stuff," demonstrating an uncanny ability to catch us in our untruths and cut away falsity. The Queen of Swords is not usually an enamored supporter, but we are better off with the Exactor than without. This supporter protects us from ourselves. This is someone who teaches us to keep promises, to do a thorough job, and to be truthful. He or she models clear communication skills and how to stand by our truth.

The Exactor is also someone who can keep us on task through setting limits and encouraging discipline.

Detractor: Critic

As a detractor the Queen of Swords dispenses criticism without compassion and often without basis in a manner that can be denigrating. The Critic may in fact be projecting self-criticism or may not be making an effort to discern the entire truth of the situation, finding it easier to make us wrong. When a Critic shows up in our lives,

Matriarch of Blades,
Native American
Tarot

our first job is to discern whether the evaluation holds an element of truth. However, we do not have to accept disparaging or destructive criticism "lock, stock, and barrel." This kind of harsh judgment can have profound, long-lasting effects on self-esteem, especially when it is directed toward children. The Critic also gives us an opportunity to ask, "How critical are we of ourselves and others?"

Queen of Swords, Thoth Tarot

Resource: Discrimination

The resource of Discrimination relates to making choices and weeding things out. This is the Exactor applied to our mental processes. When we make choices, we are using the Queen's sword.

Queen of Swords,
Spiral Tarot

Making a decision creates a direction in which our attention can be focused and our energy applied. We also use the sword of Discrimination to figure out right from wrong by analyzing the possible consequences of our actions. In addition, Discrimination can draw a line. We use this inner tool to discern and draw appropriate boundaries between ourselves and other people. Discrimination helps us avoid confusion and retain mental clarity.

Challenge: Self-Criticism

Most of us are familiar with Self-Criticism. This is the inner voice that criticizes us, judges others, and contributes to low self-esteem or feeling useless. However, is the self-critical voice ours, or is it a voice we have internalized from an important person in our life who was (or is) critical? The challenge is to ascertain the validity of the self-criticism and whether it is blown out of proportion. We need to validate our strengths and come to a realistic assessment. The inner voice that criticizes can also be directed toward others, judging them harshly. This can be disguised self-criticism projected onto an unsuspecting person outside us.

Divination Guideline

If the Queen of Swords shows up in a reading, ask yourself:

♠ Who in my life keeps me in line by holding me to the truth?

♠ How might this person help me in my given situation?

♠ Is there someone in my life who criticizes me?

♠ Am I feeling devalued by this criticism? What is my true worth?

In a reading, the Exactor can also suggest

♠ An invitation to set boundaries with self and others

♠ A period of limitation, cutting back, restriction

♠ The need for more mental clarity, decisiveness, discrimination

♠ The ability to be self-disciplined

♠ A tendency toward self-criticism and repression

♠ The possibility of being overly judgmental of self or others

The Queen of Swords Speaks

On the mountaintop amid the clouds I sit in judgment. I am the discerning mind that makes choices and decisions. I hold one hand out as a gesture of welcome. I am not all mind but human as well, even though you see only my right side, the side of reason. My crown is a wreath of butterflies. My cape is the fabric of the sky. I am sacrifice and sometimes sorrow.

In my negative aspect everything in my sight, including myself, is open to judgment. I wield the sharp and wounding sword of brutal truth and unfair criticism. I am alone and without friends.

I am true to my purpose with unwavering focus.

KNIGHT OF SWORDS

Supporter: Champion
Detractor: Rival
Resource: Insight
Challenge: Anger

Supporter: Champion

The Knight of Swords is the archetypal knight fighting on behalf of his or her liege. A Champion is someone who goes to bat for us. This supporter understands our cause, beliefs, or position and is committed to standing by us. A Champion is not a cheerleader or motivated by love. The Champion acts on our behalf because he or she believes in our cause. The Knight of Swords fights for us and supports through action.

KNIGHT OF SWORDS

Knight of Swords,
Alchemical Tarot

Interestingly, a Champion may fight for us even if we do not request or desire it. The hallmark of a champion is loyalty and a desire to make sure our side is represented. Sometimes this supporter is better placed to advance the cause than we are.

Detractor: Rival

The shadow side of the Knight of Swords is the Rival. This is an adversary who takes the opposite position from us or a nemesis whom we compete with. The Rival challenges our positions and ideas, testing the validity of our thinking. This detractor pushes us to do better, ups the ante, and calls out the best in us. A Rival may be a friend or acquaintance who plays the devil's advocate. A Rival can also be a business competitor. Unlike the King of Cups detractor, the Betrayer, whose actions may be hidden, the Rival makes his or her intentions obvious.

Resource: Insight

On the inner level the Knight of Swords represents the resource Insight. This is the strategic mind that figures the best way forward, then carries out the plan. Our inner Knight of Swords wants action and results. Therefore cunning and strategy is followed by implementation guided by the focused mind. We can also

Ritter der Schwerter
Knight of Swords

Tarot of the
Northern Shadows

use this resource to clearly communicate our position or thinking to others.

Challenge: Anger

The challenge of the Knight of Swords is Anger. In this mode we can be intolerant, contentious, argumentative, or spiteful. This is anger turned outward in active or verbal expression that is destructive and often self-serving. This destroys relationships, causes mental anguish, and perpetuates pain and suffering. This challenge is a big one on both personal and collective levels. What do we do with our rage? Can we work through it within ourselves, then express it in a way that is constructive and potentially healing?

Divination Guideline

If the Knight of Swords shows up in a reading, ask yourself:

♠ Who in my life champions my efforts in the world?

♠ How might this person help me in my given situation?

♠ Is there someone in my life whom I am competing with?

♠ How can I use this person to bring out the best in me?

In a reading, the Champion can also suggest

♠ An invitation to cross swords or compete

♠ A period of active communication and strategic planning

♠ The need for a spokesperson to state your case and represent you

♠ The ability to "go to bat" for others and give penetrating insight

♠ A tendency toward confrontation or explosive anger

♠ The possibility of being intolerant with self or others

The Knight of Swords Speaks

High above dark, swiftly moving clouds herald change. The rider with wings of passion crowning his head rides upon a horse whose hooves barely touch the ground. Out of breath, the warrior speaks:

I am intellectual fervor, the committed, persevering mind, decisive pursuit. The bridle's red heart shows my intentions. I uphold the right and the good. With the force of my support I create change and movement. I make things happen. I am the defender, committed to my position. I use cunning for those I defend. My mind is quick and strategic—readily adaptable to changing circumstance. I am not caught unaware by change but use it to my advantage.

In my negative aspect I am the challenger, the opposition. I am gleefully annoying in my persistent foiling of my foe's progress. Anger fuels my actions. My presence hampers movement. I obstruct and cause conflict.

♠

I am the dexterous mind.

PAGE OF SWORDS

Supporter: Student
Detractor: Dabbler
Resource: Curiosity
Challenge: Confusion

Supporter: Student

Recognizing a Student supporter in our life is relatively easy. He or she is thirsty for the knowledge we have and will seek us out. How does this support us? Student sup-

PAGE of SWORDS.

porters create a flow of ideas in our lives. By passing our knowledge on to them, we make space to learn more ourselves. They help keep the cycle of knowledge and learning moving. Children often fill this support role. Students ask penetrating questions, are curious, and show interest in what we have to say. They go away and assimilate or digest the information we give them, then return to ask new questions that show a deepened understanding. They help us to clarify our own thinking.

Detractor: Dabbler

Dabbler describes the shadow personality of the Page of Swords. This might be someone who flirts with a great variety of interests. The Dabbler's seeking, though, is shallow and without purpose. Accumulated knowledge remains undigested or not applied. If we have a Dabbler in our life, we may find ourselves frustrated with and drained by his or her lack of depth. This detractor asks mindless questions or repeats the same theme, never moving beyond it and exhibiting only superficial growth. This person may mirror our own lack of interest or shallow seeking. The perpetual student, dilettante, or "workshop junkie" exemplifies the Dabbler.

LIV. THE SLAVE OF THE SWORD

The Slave of the Sword, Egyptian Tarot

Resource: Curiosity

The Page of Swords as an inner resource represents our inquiring mind. Scientists, mathematicians, sociologists, and artists, among others, use the powerful mindset of curiosity to energize and focus their work, often breaking new ground in their fields simply because they wanted to know who, what, why, or how.

PAGE OF SWORDS

Page of Swords,
Tarot of Marseilles

Where could we begin asking questions or seeking knowledge? The Page of Swords represents our mind's desire and ability to learn.

Challenge: Confusion

As an inner-level challenge, the Page of Swords describes Confusion. This challenge may look like an inactive mind, one that does not bother to ask questions. The mind may be dull, uninterested from disuse, or mesmerized by television. Confusion delays action and decision and may manifest as procrastination, indifference, or ambivalence.

Divination Guideline

If the Page of Swords shows up in a reading, ask yourself:

- ♠ Who in my life is seeking knowledge from me?

- ♠ How might this person help me in my given situation?

- ♠ Is there someone in my life who has taken what I have to teach and is ready to move on?

- ♠ How might I also be stuck or confused?

In a reading, the Student can also suggest

- ♠ An invitation to teach or to learn

- ♠ A period of study and/or discipleship

- ♠ The need to learn about something new

♠ The ability to use curiosity as a guide

♠ A tendency toward confusion

♠ The possibility of not applying, assimilating, or understanding gathered information

The Page of Swords Speaks

I am high in the clouds of learning. I am the inquiring mind, the seeker of knowledge. I ask questions and play with information, seeing how it fits together. I am the young philosopher. I test my ideas in life's arena. I am assigned to ask questions and discover the capabilities of my mind. I use the sword of knowledge to direct my intellectual pursuit and clear a path for my curiosity to follow.

In my negative aspect I hate learning or am forever lost in the clouds of theory, never able to apply it to reality. I flit like a butterfly from interest to interest, never resting long enough in one place to make use of what I learn. I am the mind that prefers to wander or daydream. I have difficulty applying what I have learned.

♠

I am the student of life.

SWORD COURT CARDS: A RANGE OF DIVINATORY MEANINGS AND ASSOCIATIONS

Court Card	King	Queen	Knight	Page
Historical Person	David	Pallas	None	Hogier
Grimaud	War, supremacy	Destruction bearing fruit	Troubling events take turn for better, news of disaster	Powerlessness in the face of strong forces
Character	Man of ideas, firm, stern, wise, a pure intellect, severe, soldier, enemy	Sad, dour, sly, crafty, keen, quick, perceptive, just, graceful, fond of dancing	Active, clever, skillful, domineering, courageous, fierce	Stern, revengeful, destructive, logical, practical wisdom
Occupation	Lawyer, judge	University administrator, prime minister, president, politician, government worker	Surgeon, psychoanalyst, social worker, teacher	Spy, secret service, police, student
Psychic	Lawsuit, war	Widowhood, mourning, sterility, prudery	An enemy or spy	Bad news, delay, deceit, watch out for unforeseen messages, disturbing news, sickness, surprises
Elemental	Fire of Air	Water of Air	Air of Air	Earth of Air
Qabalistic	Chokmah in Yetzirah	Binah in Yetzirah	Tiphareth in Yetzirah	Malkuth in Yetzirah

Court Card	King	Queen	Knight	Page
Astrology	20° Taurus to 20° Gemini; May 11–June 10	20° Virgo to 20° Libra; Sept. 12–Oct. 12	20° Capricorn to 20° Aquarius; Jan. 10–Feb. 8	Dec. 22–March 20
I Ching Hexagram	32: *Héng*, Duration	28: *Ta Kuo*, Preponderance of the Great	57: *Sun*, the Penetrating, Wind	18: *Ku*, Work on What Has Been Spoiled
Tattwa	Red triangle in blue circle	Silver crescent in blue circle	Blue circle in blue circle	Yellow square in blue circle
Appearance	Dark hair and eyes, mature man	Brown hair and eyes, mature woman	Dark hair and brown eyes, young man	Boy or girl with brown hair and eyes
Psychology	*Arrien:* Passionate thinking, ambition, determination *Greer:* Established thought, ability to communicate and be analytical	*Arrien:* Mask cutter, determination to cut through roles, masks, defenses *Greer:* Channels thought, able to speak on behalf of others, sees through deceit	*Arrien:* Newly mastered intuitive, creative thinking *Greer:* Focused on making a point, committed to ideas, thoughts, philosophy	*Arrien:* Mood fighter, practical commonsense thinking, mental clarity *Greer:* Seeks justice and truth, cuts through depression, takes risks with communication
Support Role	Adviser	Exactor	Champion	Student

Sources

Historical person: *The Encyclopedia of Tarot*, Stuart R. Kaplan. Grimaud: *The Dictionary of the Tarot*, Bill Butler. Character, occupation, psychic: compilation of various authors' interpretations as found in *Dictionary of the Tarot*, Butler. Elemental: *The Golden Dawn*, Israel Regardie. Qabalistic: *Self-Initiation into the Golden Dawn Tradition*, Chic Cicero and Sandra Tabatha Cicero. Astrology: *The Book of Thoth*, Aleister Crowley. I Ching Hexagram: *Book of Thoth*, Crowley; *The I Ching*, trans. by Richard Wilhelm and Cary F. Baynes. Tattwa: *Tarot Mirrors*, Mary K. Greer. Appearance: *A Complete Guide to the Tarot*, Eden Gray. Psychology: *The Tarot Handbook*, Angeles Arrien; *Tarot for Your Self*, Mary K. Greer.

KING of PENTACLES.

QUEEN of PENTACLES

KNIGHT of PENTACLES.

PAGE of PENTACLES.

EIGHT
The Pentacle Court in the Kingdom of Power

The key words for the suit of pentacles are *power, instinct, physicality,* and *matter.* Pentacle supporters have to do with the physical level of our existence. They have to do with what we make of the matter around us—how we create it, mold it, transform it, grow it, and share it. Pentacle detractors reflect how we limit our experience in the physical world.

KING OF PENTACLES

Supporter: Mentor
Detractor: Miser
Resource: Generosity
Challenge: Greed

Supporter: Mentor

Mastery of the physical plane describes the King of Pentacles in the support role of Mentor. A Mentor is someone who has reached a level of accomplishment or skill that is recognized by others. This supporter teaches his or her craft and

KING of PENTACLES.

Roi de Deniers,
Roi de Deniers,
Oswald Wirth Tarot

acts as a career or professional role model. However, a Mentor need not be limited to the work arena. A Mentor may teach us a hobby such as music, art, or sports. Mentor supporters can be generous, magnanimous, and all-giving.

Detractor: Miser

The negative side of the King of Pentacles is the Miser. This is someone who has skill, maturity, and prosperity but will not share it. He or she hoards wealth of all kinds. This is the archetypal lonely millionaire. However, one does not have to be rich to qualify as a Miser. This detractor can show up as a boss who does not give raises or who provides an inferior work environment. This detractor chooses to withhold accessible resources that others might benefit from. The Miser challenges us to ask whether we are denying ourselves things that could otherwise make life easier, happier, or more fulfilling.

Resource: Generosity

On the inner level the King of Pentacles represents our natural aptitudes, capacity to receive, and ability to be generous. On one level this inner ally can point to areas where we possess highly developed skills. What gifts or talents have been generously bestowed upon us? Do we make something of those gifts and share them with others? On another level generosity can represent

König der Scheiben
King of Discs

King of Discs, Tarot of the
Northern Shadows

our ability to be financially abundant and productive and to share our harvest with others. This calls for letting go and giving. This resource speaks of our ability to be prosperous and successful.

Challenge: Greed

As an inner challenge, the King of Pentacles represents Greed or the excessive need to possess or experience some aspect of life. In this mode we may think that we are lacking in material possessions or feel an emptiness that cannot be satisfied no matter how much we in fact have. Greed challenges us to examine our desire to accumulate or hoard and make a realistic assessment of our needs and resources. Usually our complaint can be found in one of these areas: not enough sex, or money, or time, or love. Can we find acceptance for what we do have? Can we manage the sacrifice of giving away what we feel is scarce?

It is important to note that Greed in the form of overindulgence is the beginning point of self-destruction that is characteristic of the shadow side of the Queen of Pentacles, the next court card in this series.

Divination Guide

If the King of Pentacles shows up in a reading, ask yourself:

- ♦ Who in my life is teaching me a craft, trade, or profession?
- ♦ How might this person help me in my given situation?
- ♦ Is there someone in my life who is miserly and withholds from me?
- ♦ Does this affect how I feel about myself?

In a reading, the Mentor can also suggest

- ♦ An invitation to be generous and share your wealth
- ♦ A period of prosperity

- ◆ The need to call on a mentor to reach a specific goal

- ◆ The opportunity to teach others a craft, trade, or profession

- ◆ A tendency toward perfectionism

- ◆ The possibility of greed

The King of Pentacles Speaks

I am a force to be reckoned with. I take up space. I am not easily vanquished, and my holdings are great. I am benevolent, generous, and well loved. I am Bacchus, god of wine and physical pleasure. I provide food and shelter for many. I am commerce and trade. I promote win-win relationships. I teach others how to achieve right livelihood. I am earthy and of the people. I am mastery of physicality. The ram symbolizes my procreative force and my fertile nature of abundance.

In my negative aspect I hoard my possessions and refuse to share. I follow a win-lose approach. I am ruled by fear and am not satisfied with what I have. I always want more. I am not generous, and those around me suffer.

◆

I am stability and accomplishment.

QUEEN OF PENTACLES

Supporter: Healer
Detractor: Abuser
Resource: Self-Care
Challenge: Self-Destruction

QUEEN ofPENTACLES

Supporter: Healer

The Healer facilitates wholeness and health. A Healer may help us groom, adorn, or exercise our bodies. As a supporter the Healer helps us achieve physical integrity and balance. Most commonly this may be a body worker, massage therapist, dietician, doctor, dentist, hairdresser, physical therapist, personal trainer, or yoga teacher.

But a Healer can take other forms. For example, one man dreamed of his wife holding and caring for his intestines as he lay with his stomach wide open. Somehow this act provided him with great relief. Finally he asked her to put them back and she did. Stress is often stored in the intestines. This dream symbolically showed the dreamer how his wife played a role in relieving his stress. His psyche identified her as one of his Healers.

Detractor: Abuser

The shadow side of the Healer is the Abuser. An abuser may be someone who directly threatens our physical safety or who through self-abuse (that is, drugs, alcohol, reckless living) affects our well-being. Having this detractor in our lives challenges us to recognize how deeply his or her abuse or self-destructive behavior affects us. We may need to ask how we participate in the Abuser's destructive cycle and what we can do change in order to better care for ourselves. This Abuser may also mirror our own physical imbalance and metaphorically ask us to consider how we mistreat ourselves.

Queen of Disks,
Thoth Tarot

Resource: Self-Care

As an inner ally the Queen of Pentacles represents Self-Care, our capacity for taking care of our physical body and health. This includes knowing who our healers are and calling on them when we need to. It is surprising how many of us have difficulty looking after matters such as diet, exercise, and rest. Self-care is about knowing our body's limits and what it needs to function well and support us in the world.

Challenge: Self-Destruction

The challenge of the Queen of Pentacles is our urge toward self-destruction. If we mistreat our body long enough through overindulgence, self-neglect, physical addictions, stress, or self-deprivation, we compromise our health. This challenge calls on us to become more aware of how we use our body and any messages it may be sending us.

Priestess of Discs,
Motherpeace Tarot

What self-destructive behaviors, such as overeating, drug taking, or excessive drinking, mask difficult emotions? Are we ignoring physical pain or discomfort?

Divination Guide

If the Queen of Pentacles shows up in a reading, ask yourself:

♦ Who in my life heals or brings me comfort physically?

♦ How might this person help me in my given situation?

♦ Is there someone in my life who is abusive toward me or others?

♦ What must I do to take care of my physical and emotional health?

In a reading, the Healer can also suggest

♦ An invitation to nurture oneself

♦ A period focused on physical well-being and healing

♦ The need to pay attention to health and physical balance

♦ The ability to heal others

♦ A tendency toward self-destructive behaviors

♦ The possibility of neglecting physical health

The Queen of Pentacles Speaks

I am the healer. I am health and well-being. I am your body, the holy, earthly garment of your soul.

I am also plant, rock, tree, and creature. I am Mother Earth. I am the living, breathing form you live on. From the womb of my very being fertility abounds. My cycle brings regeneration and new life, season upon season upon season. My power is life.

In my negative aspect, I am angry at your exploitation. In my anger I storm; I become diseased. My inhabitants see themselves as separate from me, but they are not. They live, breathe, and eat me—so they will become as I, diseased and angry. They do not realize that they are the living consciousness of this planet or that through their decisions the earth—me—lives or dies.

♦

Listen to me. I am you.

KNIGHT OF PENTACLES

Supporter: Protector
Detractor: Deserter
Resource: Trust
Challenge: Neglect

Supporter: Protector

A Protector supporter offers us stability, safety, and security. He or she is our "safe port in a storm" offering food, money, shelter, clothing, or simply good companionship. When we are with a Protector we feel physically nurtured and secure. The Protector ally grounds us as an anchor holds a boat. In rough times a Protector keeps us from hitting bottom. This supporter models how to structure and securely form our lives. He or she probably has well-stocked cupboards, an emergency "nest egg," and a steady routine. The Protector demonstrates how to create abundance, physical balance, and security.

Detractor: Deserter

The shadow side of the Protector is the Deserter, who abandons responsibilities and leaves us alone feeling unsupported and unloved. The Deserter may cause us to take on life responsibilities before we are ready for them and cause low self-esteem. In this mode this detractor challenges us to create a secure base for ourselves and find outside support.

This detractor can also be someone who has withdrawn from life or relationships. His or her life is hallmarked by nar-

Knight of Pentacles,
Aquarian Tarot

row focus, rigidity, and inaction. Safety is first and foremost at the expense of growth and movement. The Deserter is often paralyzed by fear and highly values the status quo. When we are around this detractor we may feel stalled or blocked on our own path of growth.

Resource: Trust

The inner resource Trust represents our capacity to trust our survival skills and those we rely on for physical and emotional well-being. We might have all the security in the world (money, home, health) and still feel insecure, fearing we may lose it all tomorrow. The saying "Trust in Allah, but tether your camel" could well be the motto

Warrior of Shields,
Native American Tarot

for the Knight of Pentacles. It addresses the need to trust yet still do what we can to help ourselves along in the world. The Knight of Pentacles as a resource represents the ability to provide security and to be self-confident and responsible.

Prince of Disks,
Thoth Tarot

Challenge: Neglect

On the other side of the coin the inner challenge presented by the Knight of Pentacles is Neglect. Instead of being responsible, we are neglectful. We display passively abusive behavior that affects ourselves and others. This is different from the challenge of the Page of Wands, Immaturity, where responsible behavior is passed over for self-indulgent play. Neglect as it relates to the Knight of Pentacles is more of a conscious, "digging the heels in" refusal to take care of our responsibilities. This challenge calls on us to recognize what or who we are neglecting and discover our underlying motivation for this lack of caring.

Divination Guide

If the Knight of Pentacles shows up in a reading, ask yourself:

♦ Who in my life acts as a physical lifeline?

♦ How might this person help me in my given situation?

♦ Is there someone in my life who has deserted or neglected me?

♦ How can I gain a new sense of security and safety?

In a reading, the Protector can also suggest

♦ An invitation to regroup, gather resources

♦ A period of seeking financial or residential security

♦ The need for stability

♦ The ability to be grounded

♦ A tendency toward stubbornness and/or resistance to change

♦ The possibility of being narrow-minded

The Knight of Pentacles Speaks

I am security and stability. Some would call me plodding. However, I am thorough and pay attention to detail. My realm is the physical plane. I am clever with my hands and like to build structures of strength and endurance. I am methodical, and when I set my goals I steadily achieve them. I take care of those things that others do not care about, such as the plumbing. I am the practical doer.

In my negative aspect I can be heavy, slow, and burdensome. Some might feel depressed around me. I get bogged down in detail and have difficulty taking my nose from the grindstone. My efforts are laborious. I can be unmoving and stubborn, refusing to leave the structures that I have built. If I become stuck in an inner mire of turmoil, I may withdraw and desert those around me.

◆

I am a trustworthy companion. Leave your worries at the door and feel the protective safety of my presence.

PAGE OF PENTACLES

Supporter: Apprentice
Detractor: Idler
Resource: Diligence
Challenge: Inertia

Supporter: Apprentice

The Apprentice learns a craft, trade, or particular skill to put a roof overhead, food on the table, and clothes on his or her back. We teach the Apprentice career skills and skills for living.

PAGE of PENTACLES.

Page of Coins,
Tarot of Marseilles

The exchange between us and an Apprentice can also show up in the form of a patron/artisan relationship. In this mode we (the patron) support the craft of the Apprentice (the artisan) monetarily, creating a financial exchange or flow that allows the artisan to continue his or her creative work. Occasionally this card can also indicate an unborn child, that is, pregnancy. Or it might indicate someone who is dependent because of health reasons or difficult life circumstances.

As distinguished from the Page of Swords Student, the Apprentice seeks to learn specific skills related to livelihood and survival. The Student seeks information, worldly knowledge, or a philosophical understanding of life.

Detractor: Idler

The shadow side of the Page of Pentacles describes the Idler. One way this detractor may show up is as an employee or coworker who merely passes time in a job. The Idler's lack of enthusiasm and energy is marked. This can become a problem if we end up doing the work for two. This may also indicate someone who has chosen not to work and may have become dependent upon us for basic survival needs. This detractor may have the ability to make it in the world but is unwilling to make the effort. Or it could be a friend who borrows money but rarely pays it back. The Idler might also be called a freeloader, layabout, sponge, loafer, or drifter.

Resource: Diligence

As an inner resource the Page of Pentacles represents Diligence—our innate ability to handle the world and create new things in our life through hard work, skill, and perseverance. It also represents discipline and stamina as we learn skills and acquire physical resources.

LXVIII. THE SLAVE OF THE
PENTACLE

*The Slave of the
Pentacle, Egyptian
Tarot*

Sometimes the position of this card in a reading may indicate the type of skills needing to be learned. For example, if it shows up in a relationship position, then we are being asked to actively develop relationship skills.

Challenge: Inertia

We all know what it is like to have a hard time getting up in the morning or getting the energy together to get basic chores done. These are examples of Inertia, the inability to move or make progress. We just do not seem to have the energy to get out of bed or off the sofa or to make changes in our life. This challenge asks us to look at what stops us from making movement or change. Is there a fear stopping us, a belief that is self-blocking, or strong feelings that are unacknowledged? Are there health issues?

Inertia may be known more commonly as the lack of activity, but it can also refer to being incapable of changing an ongoing cycle of action. This aspect of Inertia is exemplified in the workaholic who has difficulty stopping the cycle of work to rest or enjoy recreation.

The Page of Pentacles as a challenge can also indicate skills we do not have or that are undeveloped. By developing these areas or learning new skills, we increase our understanding of the world and our ability to grow.

Divination Guide

If the Page of Pentacles shows up in a reading, ask yourself:

- Who in my life is learning a new craft or trade?

- How might this person help me in my given situation?

- Is there someone in my life who is idling, unmotivated, or benefiting from my hard work while not making an effort him- or herself?

- How might this person's attitude be blocking my progress or mirroring that attitude in me?

In a reading, the Apprentice can also suggest

- An invitation to begin a new project

- A period of learning a new skill, trade, or profession

- The need to focus on basic survival skills

- The ability to work diligently

- A tendency to display ineptitude or feel stuck

- The possibility of being without goal, direction, or motivation

The Page of Pentacles Speaks

I am the apprentice. I seek to understand my environment by using my hands and manipulating things around me. I am interested in all things material. I knit, throw pots, build, garden, brew, raise animals, and make things from the goods of the earth. I am learning how to have power in the world and gather skills to make my way.

In my negative aspect I am lazy and have high expectations. I expect to have skill and power in the world without earning it through hard work and patience. I idle away my time without direction or purpose. I have little motivation.

◆

I am the neophyte.

PENTACLE COURT CARDS: A RANGE OF DIVINATORY MEANINGS AND ASSOCIATIONS

Court Card	King	Queen	Knight	Page
Historical Person	Caesar	Rachel	Nnone	Hector
Grimaud	Possessions in a precarious state	Sale of possessions	Success due to force, perseverance, and will	Material work to ensure existence
Character	Valor, business aptitude, vanity, pride, mechanical, mathematical, dependable, family man, competent	Generous, intelligent, married woman, domesticated, hardworking, substance abuse, greatness of soul	Responsible, useful, economic, brave, fair, patient, laborious, dull	Diligent, deliberate, youth, thrift, idleness, careful, avarice
Occupation	Banker, gambler, real estate	A woman of means	Unemployed	Bookkeeper, editor, disciple, student, messenger, news agent, officer, soldier
Psychic	Wealth, luxury, success	Prosperity, illness, inheritance, happy marriage	Loan, inheritance, idleness	Application, study, scholarship, news, messages, prodigality
Elemental	Fire of Earth	Water of Earth	Air of Earth	Earth of Earth
Qabalistic	Chokmah in Assiah	Binah in Assiah	Tiphareth in Assiah	Malkuth in Assiah
Astrology	20° Leo to 20° Virgo; Aug. 11–Sept. 11	20° Sagittarius to 20° Capricorn;	20° Aries to 20° Taurus; April 11–May 10	March 21–June 20

Court Card	King	Queen	Knight	Page
I Ching Hexagram	62: *Hsiao Kuo*, Preponderance of the Small	31: *Hsien*, Influence	53: *Chien*, Development Mountain	52: *Kên*, Keeping Still,
Tattwa	Red triangle in yellow square	Silver crescent in yellow square	Blue circle in yellow square	Yellow square in yellow square
Appearance	Black hair, black eyes, swarthy skin, mature man	Black hair, black eyes, swarthy skin, mature woman	Black hair, black eyes, swarthy skin, young man	Boy or girl with black hair, black eyes, swarthy skin
Psychology	*Arrien:* The healer, diagnostician, deep commitment to health and financial well-being	*Arrien:* Exercise, health, and nutrition	*Arrien:* Physical activity, doer, builder	*Arrien:* Bearer of new life and creative projects
	Greer: Established work, ability to produce and be practical	*Greer:* Channels sensory information and practical knowledge, respect for body, food, land	*Greer:* Doing or teaching your accomplishments, committed to security, stable, reliable, stubborn	*Greer:* Seeks knowledge, experience, and new skills
Support Role	Mentor	Healer	Protector	Apprentice

Sources

Historical person: *The Encyclopedia of Tarot*, Stuart R. Kaplan. Grimaud: *The Dictionary of the Tarot*, Bill Butler. Character, occupation, psychic: Compilation of various authors' interpretations as found in *Dictionary of the Tarot*, Bill Butler. Elemental: *The Golden Dawn*, Israel Regardie. Qabalistic: *Self-Initiation into the Golden Dawn Tradition*, Chic Cicero and Sandra Tabatha Cicero. Astrology: *The Book of Thoth*, Aleister Crowley. I Ching Hexagram: *Book of Thoth*, Crowley; *The I Ching*, trans. by Richard Wilhelm and Cary F. Baynes. Tattwa: *Tarot Mirrors*, Mary K. Greer. Appearance: *A Complete Guide to the Tarot*, Eden Gray. Psychology: *The Tarot Handbook*, Angeles Arrien; *Tarot for Your Self*, Mary K. Greer.

NINE
Divination with Court Cards

This chapter presents Tarot spreads specifically designed to identify inner and outer sources of support. If you are new to the Tarot, the court card spreads in this chapter can be an easy introduction to Tarot divination.

READING COURT CARDS

There are many excellent books that deal in depth with learning to read the Tarot. Many of these are listed in the bibliography. Briefly, though, learning to read the Tarot combines study, developing intuition, self-understanding, and practice. I will discuss each of these below. In addition, I will offer general guidelines specifically addressed to reading court cards, incorporating both their inner and outer meanings, and explain what a reversed court card might signify. Lastly, I will provide a simple format for recording a reading that can be used or adapted to suit your individual style.

Study

Reading books on the Tarot is one way to begin learning how to read the cards. Researching and seeking to understand the symbols on the different cards through study or meditation can also be helpful.

Try applying your expertise in other areas, such as astrology, cooking, psychology, raising children, biology, or mathematics, to the Tarot. You will see how your other fields of experience and the Tarot interrelate. Use these other systems to describe the cards. This can help you understand them in a language you already know.

Try to "get inside" each card and allow room for the card to reveal more of itself. A card, like a dream, has many layers of meaning that can become clearer as we grow and change.

Developing Intuition

Many valid approaches to developing intuitive or psychic abilities exist. Your local bookstore will no doubt have several good books on the subject.

The Tarot itself offers a wonderful medium to begin honing your intuitive abilities. Choose a simple spread for yourself or someone else. As you look at the drawn cards, begin the intuitive process by describing one of the cards in front of you and what you know about its interpretation. More often than not your intuition will be triggered by merely describing the card. Perhaps an image will come to mind, a person, a word, or a feeling. Trust in these perceptions and let them lead you on. This begins a process somewhat akin to adding links to a chain that eventually tells a tale.

A reading always relates a true life story which unfolds as you talk about the cards. This story is not always evident at the beginning. In fact nearly every reading begins as a mystery, sometimes not revealing itself until near the end. Start by talking about each card individually; soon you will see how the cards or the energies that they are representing relate to each other and give a symbolic picture of what may be going on in the querent's life (the querent is the person asking the question of the Tarot).

Here is how a three-card reading might tell such a story. For this example I shuffled the cards, then placed three cards face down in a line left to right. Slowly, I turned each card face up. The card

Eight of Swords, Wheel of Fortune, and Knight of Pentacles, Rider-Waite Tarot

on the left showed the Eight of Swords, the middle card the Wheel of Fortune, and the card on the right the Knight of Pentacles. Now remembering that a story always has a beginning, middle, and end, I began to weave a story beginning with the card on the left.

The Eight of Swords—Here is a woman who is feeling bound and trapped and perhaps alienated from those she is close to, or out of reach of her goals (the castle in the background). She cannot see what path lies ahead and seems reluctant to move forward even though her way is not truly blocked. Wheel of Fortune—As she wrestles with her inner fears, unseen forces gather around the spinning wheel of change in the higher realms. Movement is in the air; perhaps she will find a way out of her predicament. Knight of Pentacles—Who else should appear but the knight in shining armor. He carries a pentacle, a symbol of personal power and accomplishment in the physical world. Change indeed is in the air. Our heroine may now have the vehicle (horse) and energy to accomplish her goals.

This story could be individualized by relating it in the first person and adding personal information about the querent to give it more meaning. It is surprising how much insight a simple exercise like this can provide, sometimes even days later.

Self-Understanding

When you give a reading for someone else, you have a responsibility to sift the chaff from the wheat. In other words, you need to know when you might be projecting your own desires, fears, or issues into a reading. Being aware of your own process is an important skill that contributes to being able to read cards accurately. So, along with intellectual study and exercises to develop your intuition, find a way to know yourself. Ways to stay in relationship to your inner life include journal writing, recording your dreams, meditation, psychotherapy, expressive arts—any method that keeps you in touch with your inner process.

Practice

Even if you have little formal knowledge of the Tarot and traditional methods of interpretation, experiment with giving readings for yourself. Every Tarot reader, beginner to advanced, brings a different knowledge base and life experience to inform his or her interpretation. Work with what you know and go from there. Below are a few guidelines to help you get started.

Keep the Reading Open-Ended

When doing a reading for yourself or giving one for someone else, leave the reading open-ended. Allow room for more meanings and realizations to surface for you or the querent in the time following the reading.

Seek Validation

Invite those you are reading for to either validate or contradict what you say. If they contradict you, look to see how the cards might be read differently. Ask yourself if you are involving your own agenda in the reading or if there is something you have overlooked. If you remain puzzled, continue; more likely than not the pieces will come together by the end of the reading. If not, there is likely a deeper meaning to the cards than you suspect. Look for later synchronicities (if you are the querent) in dreams and life events to clarify the meaning of the reading. Also, give yourself permission not to know and to let it remain a mystery. It seems that some readings, like dreams, are meant more for contemplation than for understanding.

Involve the Querent

Invite the people you do readings for to participate, if they are willing and comfortable with that. This is their life that you are talking about and they know far more about what is going on for them than you do. You are seeking to help them see things more clearly or in a different light, but they ultimately know what is right for them. Ask them if they have ideas about what the cards mean. Often they do and can give you deeper insight into what the cards are revealing.

Inner and Outer Levels

Reading a court card is like reading any other Tarot card. However, there are certain questions you can ask yourself when a court card shows up that often yield an immediate *aha!* Read the card as relating to both the outer and the inner; both may apply.

On the Outer Level

- Does this court card represent someone the querent knows?

- Who might this person be?

- Is this a helpful person or someone who might present an obstacle?

On the Inner Level

- Does the card represent a skill, talent, or inner resource to be used or developed in this situation?

- Does this court card represent an attitude that is self-blocking or limiting?

Reversed Court Cards

A reversed card is a card that is dealt upside down because of the way the cards are shuffled. Some people deal cards upside down but do not necessarily read them as reversed or "ill-dignified." Instead they use the card's position in a spread to signify if a reversed interpretation should be considered. A reversed interpretation, as the word implies, alters the meaning of the card, often in a more negative or problematic direction. If you decide to read the card as reversed you can use the detractor and challenge meanings of the court cards as a guide to interpretation.

However, a reversed court card can also mean that the positive aspects of the card are undeveloped, are not being used, or may be unavailable at the time of the reading. For example, the Queen of Wands in its upright position could signify that insight, self-knowledge or intuitive capacities may now be available to the querent. Whereas, if this card appears reversed it may imply that these abilities are currently unavailable, unfocused, or misguided. You may also consider whether a supporter's help is being refused, or if a resource is unacknowledged. A reversed court card might also indicate a supporter or resource that is being overused or misused.

If you choose not to assign special meanings to reversed cards in your readings, then consider the "negative" attributes of the court cards as a matter of course, especially if their position in the layout or the cards surrounding them indicate such an interpretation.

Recording a Reading

Always record your readings. You might create a Tarot journal in which you write down readings, questions, and insights. Another method I have found useful is to photograph readings.

SAMPLE FORM FOR RECORDING A READING

Date: Querent:

Question asked:

Layout used:

Diagram of cards drawn (label card "rx" for reversed):

Later synchronistic events, dreams that validate reading:

Actions taken as a result of the reading:

Results of those actions:

In the following pages are a few layouts I have used to work with the court cards. Try them for yourself or develop your own to learn more about these valuable cards.

ONE-CARD SPREAD

The One-Card spread is a quick reading that can be used for a wide variety of situations. It involves selecting only one court card that then becomes a powerful symbol and guide. This spread is useful at the beginning of a project, during a difficult transition, or if you are seeking focus and direction.

Here are some suggested questions to ask yourself during this reading. You may wish to devise your own question to suit your situation.

- What inner and outer resources do I have available to draw on in this situation?

- What support people could help me with this problem?

- Is there a detractor or challenge that needs to be addressed in this situation?

- Which court card would be the most appropriate guide during this project or transition?

- What aspect of myself am I most needing to learn about or develop in this situation?

- How can I be more supportive of (fill in name)?

- What area of support am I ignoring that needs to be made more conscious?

Instructions

Separate the court cards from the rest of the deck, shuffle them while focusing on your question. Spread the cards in front of you face down and choose one.

Interpretation

1. Look at the card and see which supporter it represents. Do you know who this person is, or who might act in this capacity for you? Is this someone you might want to ask for help? Is this a support position you do for other people? If so, is this being required of you right now? Is this an inner resource that needs to be brought forward, used, or developed? Could it be a challenge that is calling for attention? Is there something to be overcome?

2. If the interpretation does not come readily, hold this card separate from the rest of the deck for a period of time and use it as a source of contemplation.

3. Be sure to record the reading.

4. If you have an extra deck, take the equivalent card out of the second deck and put it in a prominent place where you see it every day. Take note of its influence in your life over the coming days and weeks.

Here is an example of how I have used this reading for myself as the querent. When the opportunity to do this book project came my way, I was initially daunted. The publisher's deadline was only a short while away, and I knew a great deal of work still lay before me. So, right away I decided to pull a court card as a guide to my emotional process, a point of focus and a way to get a sense of where I might find support.

The card I pulled was the King of Pentacles—Mentor. The minute I saw the card I felt relief. Somehow I no longer felt so alone or overwhelmed. Because the reading indicated that this type of support would be available to me, in the months that followed I was less hesitant to ask for help when I needed it. As a result, mentor figures played a prominent role in my life, consistently showing up (sometimes unbidden) to provide guidance and know-how. To cap it off, when I got my first look at the proposed cover of the book, I was momentarily stunned to see my court card companion, the King of Pentacles, gazing back at me. Then I laughed—of course, who else? In retrospect I recognize that the King of Pentacles also reflected the inner work that was required of me, which was developing generosity (resource of the King of Pentacles) or the capacity to share what I had learned with others.

SUPPORT SPREAD I

Support Spread I is a spread for divining how a specific person supports you. Certain people consistently support us in certain ways and are easy to spot. These people and others can also briefly offer support in ways that are less discernible. This spread helps clarify these positions and gives you insight into what kind of support a specific person might be willing to provide.

Suggested Questions

- How does (name) support me?

- What is the nature of the relationship between me and (name)?

- What is the negative aspect? Is there a lesson to be embraced?

Instructions

Separate the court cards from the rest of the deck. Shuffle them while thinking of the relationship you want to know more about. Then choose three cards and turn them over.

Interpretation

1. Look at the three cards and ask yourself how this person is supporting you in the ways described in this book. How does

this person help you see your corresponding inner resource? For example, if one of the cards is the King of Wands Spiritual Elder, how does this person bring out your Spiritual Vision? Do you feel that these positions are long-term support positions or more situational?

2.   Record your reading.

SUPPORT SPREAD II

Support Spread II is a spread for divining which support positions you fill for someone else.

Suggested Questions

- Which three support positions do I fill for (name)?

- How can I better support (name)?

- What shadow aspects do I present in this relationship?

Instructions

Separate the court cards from the rest of the deck. Shuffle them while thinking about how you relate to the person you want to know about. Then choose three cards and turn them over.

Interpretation

1.   This reading is similar to the previous one. Look at the drawn cards and ask yourself how you are a supporter for the other person as described by these three allies. How does this person respond to this support? Do you ever slip into acting as a detractor? How does the other person react when you do that? Do you feel that these positions are long-term support positions or a passing phase?

2.   Record your reading.

WHO AM I? SPREAD

The Who Am I? spread can give you insight into your gifts, strengths, or challenges for a particular function that you fill in your life, for example, as a mother, father, worker, friend, boss, or the like. It can also be used to see how others perceive you.

Suggested Questions

•   Who am I as a (name of the role)?

•   How do others perceive me in my role as (name of the role)?

Instructions

Separate the court cards from the rest of the deck. Shuffle them while thinking about your question. Then choose three cards and turn them over.

Interpretation

1. Take a look at the cards drawn and consider how they might describe you in the role named. Consider the detractor and challenge aspects of the card as well. Can you see yourself acting in the ways described? If you draw kings and queens, you know those aspects are well developed. Knights and pages may indicate developing talents.

2. Record your reading.

THREE-CARD SUPPORT SPREAD

The Three-Card Support spread is a more involved spread that uses the three levels of the Tarot—the major arcana, the numbered minor arcana, and the court cards. Using the full deck can give deeper insight into a situation, and this particular spread can also help you understand the relationship between the three modes of the Tarot.

For example, here is how the same energy, such as drug addiction, can be expressed by the three levels of the Tarot. On the transpersonal level (major arcana) we may be working with addiction (the Devil). Our lesson might be to come to terms with or remove the chains binding us to a false sense of reality. On the mundane level (minor arcana) this could show up as a Five of Pentacles (Earthly Trouble), showing financial hardship or ill health. The Queen of Pentacles on the interpersonal level (court card) describes the personas of the Healer and the Abuser. In this situation this card could represent a supporter in our lives who can help heal us of our physical addiction. It can also represent our inner challenge of Self-Destruction and/or our inner resource for self-healing, Self-Care.

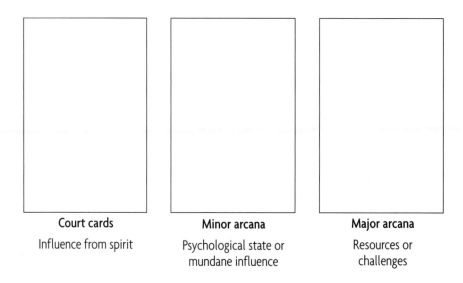

Court cards	Minor arcana	Major arcana
Influence from spirit	Psychological state or mundane influence	Resources or challenges

Suggested Questions

- What are the forces at work in this situation or relationship?

- What is going on for me or (name) right now?

- What are the choices in front of me?

Instructions

Separate the major arcana, minor arcana, and court cards into separate stacks. Shuffle each stack in turn while focusing on your question, then choose one card from each stack and turn it over.

Interpretation

1. Begin with the court card stack on the left. This card represents your inner and outer resources and talents. Take note of its suit and the supporter it represents. Ask yourself if this is someone to be sought out or if it is an inner resource that needs to be called upon. Then consider whether you (or another person) are acting out of the negative aspects of the card (detractor and/or challenge). How can you use this person or resource in your situation?

2. Next examine the minor arcana card that you pulled. This stack represents the mundane forces—everyday life experiences and psychological states. If you are familiar with the interpretations of these cards, what does that interpretation tell you about your situation? If you are not familiar with the interpretations of these cards, consider the suit and refer to the section on suits in chapter 4. Is this card the same suit as the court card? Does it have to do with your work, mental attitude, emotions, or creativity? Start to describe the card aloud to yourself. What is the scene you see in the card, what are the colors, what is the feeling of the card? See what your description brings up for you and how it might describe or shed light on your question. If you were to relate the court card and the minor arcana card to each other, how would they fit together? Can you tell a story about yourself and your situation that incorporates both cards?

3. Finally, look at the major arcana card. This card describes the influence from your higher self or spirit. You could also see it as the unconscious force at work in the situation. Again, if you are familiar with the interpretations of these cards, relate that interpretation to your question. If you are not familiar with these cards, use the technique suggested above for reading the minor arcana card, describing the card and seeing what comes up for you. The key to interpreting this position is remembering that this is the higher force at work for you right now and generally has to do with the lesson to be learned.

4. The last step is to try to relate this card back to the other two cards, linking them all together. In doing so, ponder these questions: How has the higher force (major arcana card) helped to create the situation as described by the minor arcana card? What resource or talent is the court card reminding you to use to handle the situations described by the other

cards? If you are having difficulty understanding how the cards relate to your situation, you may have to sit with the reading for a while and let it reveal itself to you over time. It might help to keep those cards in a visible place until you feel the reading is complete.

5.   Remember to record your reading.

TREE OF LIFE SPREAD

The Tree of Life layout is based on the Qabalistic Tree of Life. It is an in-depth reading using only the court cards. This is a good reading to do once a year or, at the most, every couple of months. You do not need to know the Qabalah to use this spread.

Suggested Questions

• Where are my supporters placed for the coming year?

• How are my talents focused?

• How can I apply my inner resources with regard to a specific project?

• What are my fears and concerns about what lies ahead? How might I use support to handle these and create success?

Instructions

Separate the court cards from the rest of the deck. Shuffle them while thinking of your question. Lay them out in the order indicated on the opposite page, beginning with 1, Spirit, and ending with 11, Key. You will have five cards left over. These cards are the gallery and are observers rather than participants.

1. Spirit

3. Creativity

2. Vitality

11. Key

5. Challenge

4. Opportunity

6. Identity

8. Career

7. Relationship

9. Unconscious

10. Home, Body,
Physicality

Interpretation

Take a moment to look at the reading as a whole. Are there any patterns immediately noticeable—all queens on the left pillar or no wands except in the gallery? Take note of your general impressions.

1. ***Spirit:*** Begin at the top. The Spirit position tells you your highest aspiration. In a sense this is a message from your higher self and describes the overall influence in your life right now. Look at what support this card represents. By looking at the suit, you will know the major influence at work: spirit, love, truth, or power. Then consider the supporter specifically.

   For example, if you have drawn the Page of Cups, love (cups) is the predominant theme. The Page of Cups is the Idol, so balance and harmony are a major focus in your life right now and achieving this state will enhance everything else you do. Drawing the Page of Cups here could also mean that someone who acts as an Idol for you is or will be playing a significant part in your life.

2. ***Vitality:*** This position describes the supporter who will enhance or affect your vitality. Is there a support person in your life who could help you increase your vitality? For example, suppose you draw the Queen of Pentacles, the Healer. Your vitality will be increased by using your healer allies and by focusing on your diet and exercise.

3. ***Creativity:*** It is a good idea to look at the Vitality position and this one together. If you do not have a lot of vitality or if it is being heavily focused in one direction, you will not have much energy left for creative endeavors or new activities. This position tells you how to use support to increase your creativity. How does this supporter inspire you or support you in making room for creativity? In what area is your creativity being directed? Suppose you have drawn the Queen of Wands

(Seer, Self-Knowledge) here. This could mean that your creativity could get jump-started by pulling in your Seer ally to get some insight. Or your creative energy is being directed right now toward gaining self-knowledge and achieving inner vision.

4. *Opportunity:* This position tells you from what direction opportunities will appear for you. It can also point to strengths or talents. Ask yourself how this supporter might bring you opportunity or growth. If it represents an inner resource, are you using this talent to its full potential? Do you acknowledge possessing this skill? This ally could be indicating an area in which to grow and develop. What is the shadow aspect of this card?

5. *Challenge:* In contrast to the previous position, this card describes from which direction your challenges will come. The challenge position can also tell you an area that needs to be brought back into balance. Consider the detractor and challenge attributes of the card. Why would this particular detractor represent a challenge? How does this inner challenge trip you up? Can you recognize this aspect of yourself and begin working with it? What relationship might it be talking about?

6. *Identity:* This position describes how you see yourself and how others perceive you. It can also reflect talents that are in full bloom and fully developed. It might also describe a support person that you are strongly identified with. The key to understanding this position is seeing it as yourself.

7. *Relationship:* This position indicates where your relationship energy is focused right now. It can also describe a significant relationship. This position can also point to your emotional state or mental attitude toward relationships in general.

8. ***Career:*** This position describes where your career energy is focused or what supporter can be of assistance in this area. This card may also describe your mental state or an attitude or person that is affecting your thinking and judgment.

9. ***Unconscious:*** This card describes a supporter or resource that you are largely unaware of that is asking to be brought into consciousness. The shadow/negative aspects should be considered here. What unconscious position have you taken that may undermine your efforts? What are your unconscious motivations at present? Which supporter are you not using or ignoring, to your detriment?

10. ***Home, Body, Physicality:*** What is going on with your home life? How is this supporter or detractor affecting things at home or in your physical environment? How can this inner or outer resource be used to harmonize family life? What aspect of yourself is being called on here? This position may also indicate the body. Consider if the drawn card may relate to how you or others are affecting your physical health.

11. ***Hidden Knowledge:*** This card is similar to the Unconscious position card. However, this position reveals a hidden talent or resource that is working for you in the vein of a secret admirer or a secret supporter. It can also represent a forgotten talent that can be resurrected to great benefit. What have you forgotten? Who is your fairy godmother? Can you see how this supporter might be a hidden resource working in your favor?

12. Record your reading as usual. Refer back to this reading as different areas of your life come into focus to see how the cards resonate with life events.

COURT CARD GUIDE

KINGS	King of Wands	King of Cups	King of Swords	King of Pentacles
Supporter	Spiritual Elder	Benefactor	Adviser	Mentor
Resource	Spiritual Vision	Unconditional Love	Pragmatism	Generosity
Detractor	Zealot	Betrayer	Dictator	Miser
Challenge	Illusion	Hatred	Ruthlessness	Greed

QUEENS	Queen of Wands	Queen of Cups	Queen of Swords	Queen of Pentacles
Supporter	Seer	Confidante	Exactor	Healer
Resource	Self-Knowledge	Compassion	Discrimination	Self-Care
Detractor	Pretender	Victim	Critic	Abuser
Challenge	Self-Deception	Depression	Self-Criticism	Self-Destruction

KNIGHTS	Knight of Wands	Knight of Cups	Knight of Swords	Knight of Pentacles
Supporter	Light Bringer	Lover	Champion	Protector
Resource	Creativity	Desire	Insight	Trust
Detractor	Trickster	Possessor	Rival	Deserter
Challenge	Boredom	Rejection	Anger	Neglect

PAGES	Page of Wands	Page of Cups	Page of Swords	Page of Pentacles
Supporter	Child	Idol	Student	Apprentice
Resource	Play	Harmony	Curiosity	Diligence
Detractor	Puer	Narcissist	Dabbler	Idler
Challenge	Immaturity	Jealousy	Confusion	Inertia

ASTROLOGICAL WHEEL SPREAD

The Astrological Wheel spread is similar to the Tree of Life spread but uses the astrological wheel instead as the basis for examining the different areas of our lives. The illustration of this layout shows how the wheel (a symbol for the heavens) is divided into twelve sections. These divisions correspond to the twelve houses of the zodiac that represent different life arenas.

Suggested Questions

- Which supporters are active in these areas of my life?

- Who can I draw on in the areas where I need help?

Instructions

Separate the court cards from the rest of the deck. Shuffle them while thinking of your question. When you feel ready, lay them out in the order indicated on the previous page, beginning with 1, Self, and ending with 12, Unconscious. In this reading you will have four cards left over.

Interpretation

1. As with the previous reading, take a moment to look at the reading as a whole. Do you see any patterns? If you do, note them.

2. Next, beginning with the first card (house), compare the court card drawn with the related area of your life. Remember to look at the court card both as a supporter and as an inner resource. Here is a list of what each house generally represents.

1st house	Self, Identity
2nd house	Money
3rd house	Communication
4th house	Home
5th house	Children, Play, Creativity
6th house	Work, Health
7th house	Relationship, Partnership, Marriage
8th house	Sex, Regeneration
9th house	Spiritual Fulfillment, Travel, Study
10th house	Career
11th house	Friends, Goals
12th house	Unconscious, Limitations, Spiritual State

3. If you have knowledge of astrology, you can relate the cards drawn with what you know about your natal chart and your transiting planets.

4. Record your reading.

Using court cards for divination can make us more aware of the difficult aspects of ourselves and our relationships. The next chapter suggests ways to work with the unavoidable hurdles in our life, the outer detractors and inner challenges.

TEN

Court Cards
Cast a Shadow

Once the court card support roles become familiar, the shadow side of these cards can be worked with in more depth.

We live with challenging aspects of others and ourselves every day. For example, maybe we tend to be critical, or perhaps victimized, or we live with someone who is stubborn or deceitful. Alternatively, at work we may be faced with a boss who competes with or ridicules us. This chapter offers a starting point for changing difficult behavior and relationship patterns.

THE **DEVIL**

THE SHADOW SIDE OF COURT CARDS

People in our life whom we might call "the bane of our existence" usually tend to throw us off balance or make us feel uncomfortable. Their influence varies, but typically detractors can make us feel worthless, powerless, used, vulnerable, angry, depleted, defensive, overly responsible, indecisive, or incompetent.

Humanity's Dual Nature Is Revealed—The Devil, Alchemical Tarot

Detractors can also draw from us instinctive responses or "knee-jerk" reactions that can be related to the court card challenges. For example, we have just discovered that our lover is cheating on us (Betrayer). We might drown our sorrows (Self-Destruction), go on a shopping spree (Greed), plan revenge (Anger), feel powerless (Depression), or turn green (Jealousy). You can probably predict what combination of reactions you would have. In court card terms we have responded to a detractor with our own challenging behavior.

One way of averting this scenario is to recognize our inner experience (feelings and thoughts) before proceeding with the knee-jerk reaction—that is, make the unconscious process conscious. We have the opportunity to make choices about our response that will in the end strengthen us rather than bring us down. Also, if we are able to circumvent our instinctive urge, the other person has a greater chance of acknowledging his or her part in the problem, the situation does not escalate, and we avoid wallowing around in our own negative patterns.

DISPELLING THE SHADOW

There are times, however, when our best efforts cannot accomplish this Herculean task of perception, self-knowledge, and self-discipline. We have indulged our passions and have fallen into the abyss of shadow. Now we must find a way to regain balance. Here is how the court cards can help.

Each shadow side of a court card can be worked with or counterbalanced by the harmonizing influence of another court card. For example, if I recognize that I am being intolerant and critical of others (challenge of the Queen of Swords), I identify supporters or resources that might help transform my feelings, thoughts, or impulses. Then, through seeking out the appropriate support or meditating on the harmonizing court card, I might find a way out of my critical persona.

Whichever court cards we choose to harmonize a shadow are unique to us and may change from situation to situation. In other words, if I am feeling trapped (Queen of Cups: Victim) and stuck in my feelings of helplessness, to get myself out I might try bringing in the energy of the Adviser (King of Swords) to gain intellectual understanding of the situation and to develop options. Someone else might seek out a Healer to bring in new physical energy to help ease the sense of depletion.

You can use the worksheet below together with the charts that follow to look at how you might use the positive aspects of the court cards to balance out the negative. Think of a current situation where you are struggling and link it to a court card detractor or challenge. Then contemplate the possible ways you could change things by bringing in a different focus, perspective, or supporter as represented by a court card supporter or resource.

Once you have this information, you can utilize the meditation methods described in the following chapters to even greater benefit.

DETRACTOR AND CHALLENGE HARMONIZER WORKSHEET

Detractor/Challenge	Harmonizing Court Card	Harmonizing Attributes
King of Wands Zealot, Illusion		
Queen of Wands Pretender, Self-Deception		
Knight of Wands Trickster, Boredom		
Page of Wands Puer, Immaturity		
King of Cups Betrayer, Hatred		
Queen of Cups Victim, Depression		
Knight of Cups Possessor, Rejection		

Detractor/Challenge	Harmonizing Court Card	Harmonizing Attributes
Page of Cups Narcissist, Jealousy		
King of Swords Dictator, Ruthlessness		
Queen of Swords Critic, Self-Criticism		
Knight of Swords Rival, Anger		
Page of Swords Dabbler, Confusion		
King of Pentacles Miser, Greed		
Queen of Pentacles Abuser, Self-Destruction		
Knight of Pentacles Deserter, Neglect		
Page of Pentacles Idler, Inertia		

COURT CARD SUPPORTERS AND RESOURCES

Court Card	Supporter	Resource
King of Wands	Spiritual Elder	Spiritual Vision
Queen of Wands	Seer	Self-Knowledge
Knight of Wands	Light Bringer	Creativity
Page of Wands	Child	Play
King of Cups	Benefactor	Unconditional Love
Queen of Cups	Confidante	Compassion
Knight of Cups	Lover	Desire
Page of Cups	Idol	Harmony

Court Card	Supporter	Resource
King of Swords	Adviser	Pragmatism
Queen of Swords	Exactor	Discrimination
Knight of Swords	Champion	Insight
Page of Swords	Student	Curiosity
King of Pentacles	Mentor	Generosity
Queen of Pentacles	Healer	Self-Care
Knight of Pentacles	Protector	Trust
Page of Pentacles	Apprentice	Diligence

COURT CARD DETRACTORS AND CHALLENGES

Court Card	Detractor	Challenge
King of Wands	Zealot	Illusion
Queen of Wands	Pretender	Self-Deception
Knight of Wands	Trickster	Boredom
Page of Wands	Puer	Immaturity
King of Cups	Betrayer	Hatred
Queen of Cups	Victim	Depression
Knight of Cups	Possessor	Rejection
Page of Cups	Narcissist	Jealousy
King of Swords	Dictator	Ruthlessness
Queen of Swords	Critic	Self-Criticism
Knight of Swords	Rival	Anger
Page of Swords	Dabbler	Confusion
King of Pentacles	Miser	Greed
Queen of Pentacles	Abuser	Self-Destruction
Knight of Pentacles	Deserter	Neglect
Page of Pentacles	Idler	Inertia

SHADOW SPREAD

You can also use the court cards as an oracle to point you in the direction of healing. The following spread is intended to offer resources for working with a given shadow. The resources may be people in your life or within yourself.

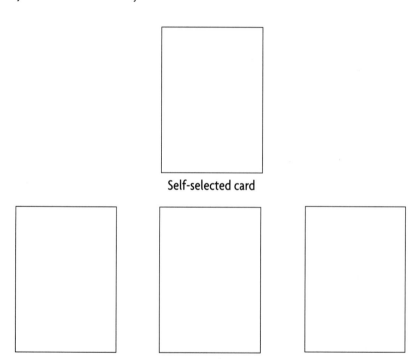

Self-selected card

Instructions

Separate the court cards from the rest of the deck. Select the court card that best represents the detractor or challenge that you are faced with. Place it faceup before you.

Shuffle the remaining court cards and select three cards. Place them below the card you have already chosen.

Interpretation

1. Notice which suits have been drawn. Does one suit dominate? This may give a good indication of what can help in the situation: spirit, love, knowledge, or power.

2.   Next, notice the different levels of royalty. This may also shed some light. If you have lots of pages, perhaps you are needing to learn something new. Or if you have drawn several kings, you may need to exercise maturity and leadership. Queens look within, knights take action.

3.   Finally, look at the specific support roles. Try to see how the energy they represent may help in your situation. Also take note of specific people they might be in your life. Perhaps these individuals have something to offer you in this situation.

4.   Make sure to record your reading

In the next chapter we go deeper still to meet the energies of the court cards on the inner planes.

ELEVEN

Meditation and the Court Cards

Divination is the act of seeking communication with a divine source. That is the goal with techniques such as meditation, pathworking, and ritual magic. When we enter meditation, follow a pathworking, assume a god form, or conduct a ritual, we seek a direct experience of the divine, a numinous or otherworldly encounter. The tools we employ are the creative imagination, intention, myth, and symbol. Such contact with Divinity enhances our personal growth and can cause material and/or perceptual change.

Meditation and pathworking methods to facilitate such communication are described below. In the following chapter, a guided pathworking is offered as an additional avenue for exploration. One word of caution: *When using the court cards in the following exercises, we are invoking only the positive, supporting, and resourceful aspects of the cards.* As William Gray states in his book *Magical Ritual Methods,* "Undesirable traits of human nature form no part of the Plan for the Innerworld outlined by the Tarots. The Court cards therefore only offer us a choice of personalities suitable for souls aspiring toward betterment of their being."[1]

MEDITATION

Meditation techniques in the Western Mysteries generally, but not always, involve the intentional use of the creative imagination and are considered magical practices by most followers of the Western esoteric traditions. During meditation we seek to purposely create images within the mind to cause changes in consciousness and sometimes circumstances. For our purposes we will define *magic* as our effort to mediate between our inner and outer selves. To quote William Gray once more, magic is "man's most determined effort to establish an actual working relationship through himself between inner and outer states of being."[2]

Preparation for Meditation

Here are a few basic requirements for meditating:

- A comfortable chair or cushion for sitting on

- A set period of time (fifteen minutes to half an hour) with no distractions

- A dimly lit room

- A rested body

- An alert mind

- Inner balance (it is best not to go into this sort of meditation session angry or upset. Write in a journal beforehand. Exercising before meditation can also be centering)

- A clear intention or focus for your meditation

To begin, select a time when you are confident you will not be interrupted. Use a comfortable chair but not one in which you could easily fall asleep. Make sure your feet can touch the ground. Have the room at a reasonable temperature and neither in total darkness nor glaringly bright. Have a notebook and pen ready for recording your experience after completing the meditation. Before you begin, record the time.

When you feel ready, seat yourself, close your eyes, and relax. Start with your feet. Let the muscles soften. Next relax your legs, your torso, your arms and hands. Consciously relax each part of your body. Relax your neck and head, especially your face and your forehead. Let your tongue rest lightly against the roof of your mouth and let your jaw relax.

Now turn your attention to your breath. Intentionally slow your breathing and make your inhalations slightly deeper and your exhalations longer. Do ten of these rhythmic breaths. When you count the tenth breath, begin to focus on the topic of your meditation.

STEPPING INTO A COURT CARD

Here is a method that other Tarot writers, including Mary Greer, William Gray, and Dolores Ashroft-Nowicki, have used with the major arcana applied specifically to the court cards. Before you step into a court card in meditation you will want to take some time to look carefully at the details of the card, committing them to memory if possible. Try looking at the card, then closing your eyes and visualizing it with your mind's eye. Do not worry if the image is not clear. Visualizing with inner sight takes practice, and some people are inherently better at it than others.

Next consider what you want from the experience. Did this court card come up in a reading in a way you did not understand? Are you asking for clarity or more information? There are many avenues for exploration; be clear in your intention.

Instructions

When you feel prepared, begin the preliminary relaxation and rhythmic breathing and start focusing on your meditation topic. Picture the chosen court card in your imagination. When the image is steady, walk into the card.

Notice what is around you. What is the weather like? What emotions are you feeling? What is the ambiance or atmosphere? Then move your attention onto the specific court card figure. Open yourself to receive communication. You may have a question for the figure, such as: What message do you have for me? What can I learn from you? Who are you? If you have a question, ask it, then become receptive and wait to see if a response occurs. The response might not be in words. So be patient and pay close attention.

When you have received a response and the interaction feels complete, give thanks, walk back out of the court card scene, and return to normal consciousness. Record your experience.

FOCAL-POINT MEDITATION

Using a focal point for meditation employs a slightly different type of skill. Instead of directing your attention toward a visual image, you focus on a sentence or phrase that you have chosen that relates to the court card you have either randomly or purposefully selected to work with. This sentence may be one that you would like further understanding of or that you think would be helpful to your particular situation.

Sentences, phrases, words may be taken, for example, from the descriptions of the court cards in this book or from other sources. Or you might use a phrase from the *I Ching* that resonates with the court card in question.

Instructions

Prepare for meditating. Relax and breathe, then hold the sentence or phrase in your mind. Repeat it silently within; see what associations come up. Follow them if they seem fruitful, or go back to the original sentence and contemplate it further. Roll the sentence or phrase around in your mind. Sometimes realizations and insights come immediately; other times it can take several meditation sessions to move deeply into the meditation topic. Be patient. End when you feel satisfied with your exploration of the topic or have an inner sense of completion. Record your experience and associations when done.

ASSUMING A COURT CARD PERSONALITY

The purpose in this exercise is to experience the *positive* aspects of a court card through the active imagination. This exercise can be used when you want to develop or activate an inner resource, such as Compassion, Generosity, or Self-Care. Through this experience you get a felt sense of these inner strengths and are later able to draw on them. Two methods are given below. The first is a method described by William Gray in his book *Magical Ritual Methods*.[3] He emphasizes the importance, once having assumed the personality, of being able to set it aside afterward.

Method 1

Select the court card personality you wish to assume. This can be done purposely or at random. Take the card you've chosen or pick one randomly from the deck and turn it right side up before you. The rest of the deck remains facedown. As you turn the card over you say, "In," and let yourself become one with the court card personality, as if taking on a role for a play. When you have experienced enough, turn the card facedown on top of the deck and say, "Out." Return to normal consciousness.

Method 2

Follow the instructions on page 167 for stepping into a court card. Once you have encountered the court card personality, imagine the person turning so his or her back is toward you. Slowly walk into the figure's form. Notice the feel of your body—your thinking and feeling and what you are seeing. When you have experienced enough, back out of the form and step out of the card, returning to normal consciousness.

AN INTRODUCTION TO PATHWORKING

I suspect that the magical technique of pathworking (a guided visualization of sorts) is as ancient as our ability to imagine. However, Dolores Ashcroft-Nowicki, a modern adept of the Western Mysteries, states that as a formal magical technique the history of pathworking may go back as far as Chaldea, ancient Greece, and Egypt.[4] Today pathworking remains a cornerstone in the training regime of students within the Western Mysteries. Pathworking, or "scrying in the spirit,"[5] opens a portal into the inner realms of the psyche and beyond. It has the potential to cause change on many levels.

In practical terms, pathworking consists of sitting in a chair, closing your eyes, and following a carefully constructed scenario with your creative imagination—visualizing in as much detail as possible a series of events as they unfold in front of your mind's eye. You may either simply observe or take part in the inner drama. Pathworkings can be developed from a variety of sources, including myths, fairy tales, poetry, mystical literature, historical events, or science fiction.

Each pathworking, like a story, has a beginning, a middle, and an end. During the working you keenly observe your surroundings and employ all your senses to notice color, sound, smell, temperature, and taste. Feelings, thoughts, or "aha!"s that emerge at different junctures are significant to note too. One of the most important rules of the working is to stick to the planned scenario without deviation. This can be difficult, as spontaneous images, feelings, and events will occur. The trick is to maintain the momentum of the working while taking careful note of the outer effects for future reference, for they are often the key to further insight. At a later date you might follow up the pathworking with meditation sessions devoted to contemplating the unusual occurrences or symbols encountered during the pathworking.

Upon completion, immediately write up your experience. As with a dream, pathworking material is easily forgotten and lost if not recalled and recorded right away. Ground yourself afterward with some food or a practical activity, such as washing the dishes.

In the following chapter the Four Kingdoms, One Road pathworking can be used to experiment with the techniques presented in this chapter.

TWELVE

Four Kingdoms, One Road

This final chapter contains a pathworking that has evolved through personal meditation. I offer it as an experiential encounter with the Tarot court. It is also a template to be developed and personalized as you further explore the inner realms of the Tarot.

Before conducting the pathworking in a formal way, carefully read it several times, perhaps even over several days. Imagine it in your mind's eye, using these preliminary readings like a dress rehearsal. It might be helpful to tape-record the working and use it to guide the actual pathworking session. Then when you feel prepared, review the instructions in the previous chapter and proceed with the working. Upon completion, write down your experience and the insights gleaned.

The Journey Begins—
Ace of Coins,
Alchemical Tarot

A PATHWORKING:
FOUR KINGDOMS, ONE ROAD

Imagine yourself in a familiar glade of trees. You walk among them following a deer trail.

Just ahead one tree stands out for its size and beauty. It seems older than the others. As you move closer you see a door in its trunk. . . . Now, standing directly in front of the tree, you trace with your finger a large quartered circle carved roughly into the heavy wooden door. In each quarter of the circle is a symbol. In the bottom left quarter is a wand; moving clockwise to the next quarter is a sword, then a pentacle, and last a cup.

You try to open the door but it is locked. You walk clockwise around the tree, curiously looking for another way in. As you make a full circle you notice a key on a faded red cord hanging on a nail in the trunk. You take the key and try it in the lock. The door opens; you put the cord with the key around your neck and move inside with only the slightest apprehension. The door closes and seals you in complete darkness.

You stand there quietly acclimating to what feels surprisingly like a cave. The sound of trickling water reaches your ears, and then suddenly someone near you clears his throat. You hear the scratch of a match, and the face of a small, craggy man comes into view. In full upright position he barely reaches your hip. As he fidgets to light a lantern, he asks what your business is. You respectfully tell him that you are looking for a way to the Four Kingdoms. He nods, grumbling that he is not so sure he is up for much more of this job, but says to follow him.

You ask yourself, "Follow him where, for Pete's sake? We're inside a tree." But you decide there is no time for rationality. Shrugging, you hurry to catch up with him. He has headed to the left and you follow this unexpectedly spry man down a narrow path flanked by sheer rock walls. The trickling sound you heard earlier grows louder. Now you see the spring ahead on the left. Water flows in a gentle but steady stream through a crack in the rock, pooling in a natural basin below. Your guide says for you to stop and bathe. He hands you a cotton towel, a clean white robe to change into, and a simple pair of sandals. He leaves you to it. You fold your clothes and place them on a shelf carved out of the stone and then wash. . . .

Once you are robed you continue down the path, heading toward the light of the resting lantern. Your guide greets you and says it is not too much farther. Now he heads to the right and then disappears around a bend. You clear the bend but see no trace of him. Puzzled, you stop. Then to your relief you once again hear him clear his throat. To your right is a narrow break in the stone wall. You slip between the stones and follow him on an even narrower path that zigs and zags through a succession of standing stones.

Finally he stops and says he can go no farther and that you must proceed alone. From around the next towering boulder the light of day penetrates the darkness. He hands you a leather pouch. Within it, he says, is all you need to pass into the Four Kingdoms. You take the satchel and slip the strap over your head and under one arm, carrying the pouch securely. You bid him good-bye and thank him. He says he will be here upon your return. You move forward past the last stone and find yourself in bright daylight on a wide, tree-lined footpath.

You look around and quickly recognize that the only direction of travel is straight ahead, away from the rocky nook sheltering the cave from which you emerged. You walk on, enjoying the light and warmth, wondering what adventures await you. In the distance appears a fork in the road.

Your feet finally bring you to the split in the path, where a monolith rises from the earth. Engraved on its face are words in a language foreign to you. At its base is a perfectly spherical stone about a foot in diameter, and on the ground before it, two parallel indentations, patches of earth worn away by the knees of fellow travelers. You are drawn, like those pilgrims before you, to kneel on the ground in front of the two stones. You close your eyes and place your hands on the smooth granite sphere. Calm and inner quiet envelop you. You contemplate the reason for your journey and what it is you hope to discover or gain from your experience. . . . Then words of intent and meaning well up from your depths and pass from your lips. . . .

As the last words are spoken, you notice a nearly imperceptible change in the air, and you realize your hands no longer rest on the spherical stone at the crossroads but now grip the edges of a flat object about eight inches round. You open your eyes, only to see your own reflection in a gilt-edged mirror. Take note of what you see. . . .

Your attention now moves to your immediate environment. You notice that you are kneeling on an intricately woven carpet just big enough for the task. It rests on an elegant stone-tiled floor.

You raise your head and behold the soft form of a crowned woman standing before you. Then you hear her melodic voice welcoming you and asking you to rise. Carefully you stand, still holding the mirror.

She asks, "What desire or matter of the heart has brought you here?" You tell her. . . . She may wish to reply; listen carefully. . . . Then she reaches toward you and you pass the mirror to her. She says, "Let us hope that what you seek can be found here."

She moves to the center of the large hall, where there is an altar about waist high and eighteen inches across. She places the mirror in the center of the altar to join a number of other items: a sword in the east, a wand in the south, a silver chalice in the west, and a small shiny piece of black stone etched with the symbol of a pentacle in the north. Through the domed glass ceiling above, sunlight refracts into jewels of fiery light that glimmer on these sacred implements.

You now observe your surroundings. The room is entirely circular. In each of the four directions stand two raised thrones, eight in all. Colorful stained glass windows are set in the semiquarters between each pair of seats. Two additional chairs stand below the southeast window. In the northwest, across from these chairs, is a door that leads to the garden. The door is attended by the Knight of Pentacles.

The thrones are occupied by the kings and queens of the four

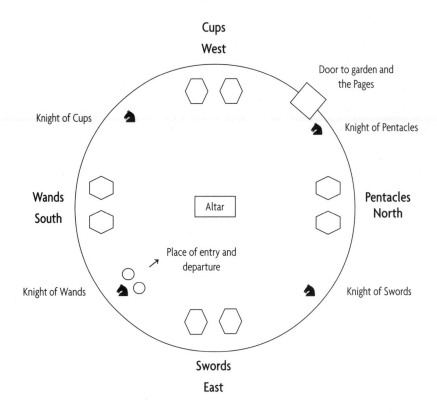

Tarot kingdoms. The King and Queen of Swords nod to you in greeting from the east. In the south the King and Queen of Wands smile warmly in your direction. The King of Cups, temporarily on his own in the west, rises and gives you a gracious bow of welcome. And last, the King and Queen of Pentacles hail you from the north. The three remaining knights stand in the other semiquarters.

The Queen of Cups now comes around the altar to your side and escorts you to one of the unoccupied chairs in the southeast, just behind you. She proceeds to her place in the west and takes her seat. The Knight of Wands now comes before you. He asks, "Who in the present company do you wish to speak with? Or perhaps there is some other way the Tarot court might serve you." You answer him. . . . He will escort any of the court members (excepting the pages) to the empty seat next to you or take you to the quarter of the one you wish to speak to.

But before he does, the Queen of Pentacles rises and also extends an invitation. She says, "The gardens outside are quite breathtaking; please feel free to wander through them and enjoy. If you wish, our knight who guards the door to the garden will escort you. He can also take you to meet with any of the pages. They can be found in the gardens. If you would rather greet them here, he will bring them to you. Just let him know your wishes." You thank her. Take some time now to seek what you have journeyed for. . . .

Finally you feel finished and return to stand on the small woven carpet. The Queen of Wands retrieves the gilt-edged mirror from the altar. Then she and the Queen of Swords come to stand in front of you. The Queen of Swords asks if your journey has brought you knowledge. You answer her and ask any remaining questions you have. . . . Listen for a response from either queen. . . . After a brief moment the Queen of Wands hands you the mirror; you kneel and look again into its depths. Take note of what you see. . . . Your eyes grow heavy and close. . . .

You become aware of a change. Your eyes open. You are back at the crossroads, with your hands upon the spherical stone. You slowly rise and make your way back to the standing stones. The little man meets you just behind the first boulder that separates light from dark, and you return the way you came, exchanging your clothes at the small pool. You thank him, unlock the door, and emerge from the tree. Place the key back on the nail. Walking away from the tree, you return to your own time and place.

Afterword

My aim in writing this book has been to give the "people cards" fresh meaning and provide a practical method of interpretation that improves lives and relationships. This unique support-based approach has focused on identifying the myriad ways that people relate to and support one another. It also recognizes individual traits and qualities that affect our relationships and sense of personal fulfillment. I hope that this knowledge may increase the reader's confidence to reach out for support and to call on inner reservoirs of strength.

Given the extent to which most of us are embroiled in a wide variety of relationships that often define our life, it has become apparent to me that the court cards may be the most useful of the deck. They give us information that can immediately and readily improve our daily living and emotional well-being.

Seen in this light, the court cards' mundane function and usefulness seems obvious and in keeping with its place in the minor arcana, the lesser mysteries. I propose, though, that the court cards in fact act as a bridge between the major arcana (the greater mysteries) and the minor arcana. The Tarot court, like humanity itself, seems to have a foot in two worlds: the physical world and the world of spirit. The same support-based principles that apply in our day-to-day existence also apply in the world of the greater mysteries.

Our supporters extend beyond the corporeal. For instance, a variety of nonphysical entities might serve as allies when approached carefully and thoughtfully. Elementals (beings of the subtle elemental world such as gnomes, undines, sylphs, and salamanders) or angelics (archangels on down) might be invited to help through talismanic magic or ritual. Ancestral forces, which play a large role in ancient Celtic and Native American traditions, present another potential resource that can be accessed through various ritual practices. Western magical techniques used in combination with the court cards offer fruitful areas of investigation within the spiritual realm.

No longer arcane and enigmatic images on dog-eared cards, for me the Tarot court card figures represent dynamic and powerful archetypal forces. They embody and communicate primordial patterns of relationship and personal expression, reflecting a perennial wisdom that reverberates through all of manifestation.

COURT CARD QUICK REFERENCE GUIDE

The following information is summarized in the Court Cards at a Glance table on page 189.

King of Wands

Supporter: Spiritual Elder
Spiritual teacher, sage, guru, shaman, magus, visionary, guide. One who shines light on a situation with spiritual knowledge.

Detractor: Zealot
Imposes his or her spiritual viewpoint upon us.

Resource: Spiritual Vision
Our ability to perceive realities beyond our physical senses and to understand our existence in the context of a greater plan.

Challenge: Illusion
Grandiosity regarding our spiritual mission or stage of personal evolution.

Queen of Wands

Supporter: Seer
Guides us toward self-knowledge. Looks to our core and holds a mirror for us to see our reflection.

Detractor: Pretender
Takes advantage of his or her intuitive abilities to manipulate others for personal gain. Blocks the path to self-knowledge.

Resource: Self-Knowledge
Our ability to know who we are and to discover what lies beneath the persona we present to the world.

Challenge: Self-Deception
Self-delusion, pretense. We may be convinced we are someone we are not.

Knight of Wands

Supporter: Light Bringer
Brings lightness to our life through humor, inspiration, optimism, and creativity.

Detractor: Trickster
Avoids making promises and slips away when we try to hold him or her accountable. Slippery, elusive, manipulative.

Resource: Creativity
Our capacity to be inspired, have new ideas, and follow through with their implementation or artistic expression.

Challenge: Boredom
Creative frustration, inadequate expressive outlets. Impatience.

Page of Wands

Supporter: Child
The epitome of enlightenment. Inspires us with his or her idealism, curiosity, zest for life, and playfulness.

Detractor: Puer
Someone who refuses to grow up and accept the responsibilities of adult life.

Resource: Play
Our ability to have fun and bring excitement into our lives.

Challenge: Immaturity
We avoid responsibility and are unable to acknowledge the impracticality of cherished hopes, desires, or ideals.

King of Cups

Supporter: Benefactor
Loves us unconditionally.

Detractor: Betrayer
Someone who violates our trust.

Resource: Unconditional Love
Our ability to be emotionally open and deeply accept others and ourselves despite shortcomings; the ability to forgive.

Challenge: Hatred
Our heart is closed. We have created a wall of separation, alienation, and a state of noncommunication. Wounded.

Queen of Cups

Supporter: Confidante
Empathic to our situation. The ideal of a friend.

Detractor: Victim
Feels victimized by the world or by those close to him or her. Someone with few boundaries.

Resource: Compassion
Our ability to empathize and understand. Ability to honestly express feelings with integrity.

Challenge: Depression
Feeling lost or numb; difficulty accessing and expressing the depths of emotion churning within.

Knight of Cups

Supporter: Lover
A lover or something we have passion for. We feel vibrant and excited.

Detractor: Possessor
Someone whose passion has become self-serving, insensitive, or possessive. The addicted lover.

Resource: Desire
Our ability to love someone passionately or live our life with exuberance and joy.

Challenge: Rejection
Our tendency to reject what we feel we cannot have or do not deserve. It is not good enough for us.

Page of Cups

Supporter: Idol
In this person's presence we experience a heightened pleasure of mind, spirit, or sensation. He or she gifts us with a sense of balance and serenity.

Detractor: Narcissist
This person is preoccupied with his or her outer appearance and image and makes little room for us in his or her life.

Resource: Harmony
Our ability to be emotionally balanced and open to new relationships.

Challenge: Jealousy
Insecurity is displayed through jealousy and selfishness.

King of Swords

Supporter: Advisor
Has answers to our questions. Has an intellectual understanding of the world that makes him or her an excellent resource when we need pragmatic solutions.

Detractor: Dictator
Has excellent analytical skills but leaves out the human element when making decisions. Someone who tries to dictate how we act, think, or feel.

Resource: Pragmatism
Our ability to be mentally determined and analytical.

Challenge: Ruthlessness
We coldly deny our feelings or desires as we live our life. We judge them to be impractical, childish, or far-fetched.

Queen of Swords

Supporter: Taskmaster
Someone who "calls us on our stuff" and has an uncanny ability to catch us in our large or small untruths.

Detractor: Critic
Criticizes us without compassion and sometimes without basis. Denigration.

Resource: Discrimination
Our ability to make choices, see right from wrong, and keep mental clarity.

Challenge: Self-Criticism
The inner voice that criticizes ourselves and judges others.

Knight of Swords

Supporter: Champion
Goes to bat for us. Understands our cause or position and actively supports us. Someone well placed to advance our cause.

Detractor: Rival
Takes an opposite position from us or competes with us. His or her presence tests us and sometimes the validity of our thinking.

Resource: Insight

The strategic mind that crystallizes options and plans the best way forward. Our ability to use cunning and communicate our stance clearly.

Challenge: Anger

Intolerance, spite. We are contentious and argumentative. Expression that is destructive or self-serving.

Page of Swords

Supporter: Student

Creates a flow of ideas in our lives. By passing our knowledge on to him or her, we make space to learn more ourselves.

Detractor: Dabbler

Flirts with a great variety of interests superficially. Filling in time, shallow and without purpose.

Resource: Curiosity

Our ability to ask questions and be inquisitive.

Challenge: Confusion

An inactive mind that does not bother to ask questions. Dull, uninterested, confused. Procrastination, indifference, ambivalence.

King of Pentacles

Supporter: Mentor

Someone who has mastery of a craft and is able to pass on his or her knowledge to us. Career role model. Accomplished and prosperous in the world.

Detractor: Miser

Has skill, maturity, and prosperity but will not share it.

Resource: Generosity

Our ability to be prosperous and share it with others. Also, our ability to have mastery of a skill or profession.

Challenge: Greed
We will not share. Attached, grasping, acquisitive.

Queen of Pentacles

Supporter: Healer
Someone who helps us achieve physical balance, health, and wholeness.

Detractor: Abuser
Someone who mirrors disease and imbalance through destructive habits or behaviors.

Resource: Self-Care
Our ability to take care of our physical body and health.

Challenge: Self-Destruction
Our possibly unconscious urge toward self-destruction.

Knight of Pentacles

Supporter: Protector
Someone who grounds us, makes us feel safe and secure. A role model for how to structure our life in a solid and secure fashion.

Detractor: Deserter
Abandons responsibilities and leaves us exposed. Withdrawn, narrowly focused, and rigid.

Resource: Trust
Our capacity to trust our survival skills and trust those we rely on for physical and emotional health.

Challenge: Neglect
Passively abusive behavior that affects ourselves and others.

Page of Pentacles

Supporter: Apprentice
Someone who learns a craft or trade from us, or someone who is dependent because of health reasons or difficult life circumstances.

Detractor: Idler
Passes time in a job, or someone who chooses not to provide for him- or herself.

Resource: Diligence
Our innate ability to handle the world and create new things in our life through hard work, skill, and perseverance.

Challenge: Inertia
Inability to move or make progress. Self-blocked, fear ridden.

COURT CARDS AT A GLANCE : SUPPORTERS, RESOURCES, DETRACTORS, AND CHALLENGES

KINGS	King of Wands	King of Cups	King of Swords	King of Pentacles
Supporter	Spiritual Elder	Benefactor	Adviser	Mentor
Resource	Spiritual Vision	Unconditional Love	Pragmatism	Generosity
Detractor	Zealot	Betrayer	Dictator	Miser
Challenge	Illusion	Hatred	Ruthlessness	Greed
QUEENS	Queen of Wands	Queen of Cups	Queen of Swords	Queen of Pentacles
Supporter	Seer	Confidante	Exactor	Healer
Resource	Self-Knowledge	Compassion	Discrimination	Self-Care
Detractor	Pretender	Victim	Critic	Abuser
Challenge	Self-Deception	Depression	Self-Criticism	Self-Destruction
KNIGHTS	Knight of Wands	Knight of Cups	Knight of Swords	Knight of Pentacles
Supporter	Light Bringer	Lover	Champion	Protector
Resource	Creativity	Desire	Insight	Trust
Detractor	Trickster	Possessor	Rival	Deserter
Challenge	Boredom	Rejection	Anger	Neglect
PAGES	Page of Wands	Page of Cups	Page of Swords	Page of Pentacles
Supporter	Child	Idol	Student	Apprentice
Resource	Play	Harmony	Curiosity	Diligence
Detractor	Puer	Narcissist	Dabbler	Idler
Challenge	Immaturity	Jealousy	Confusion	Inertia

COMPARISON OF COURT CARD TITLES

Deck	Court Card Titles			
Rider-Waite	King	Queen	Knight	Page
Marseilles	King	Queen	Knight	Page
Hanson-Roberts	King	Queen	Knight	Page
B.O.T.A.	King	Queen	Knight	Page
Northern Shadows	King	Queen	Knight	Page
Sacred Rose	King	Queen	Knight	Page
Aquarian	King	Queen	Knight	Page
Pythagorean	King	Queen	Knight	Page
Thoth	Knight	Queen	Prince	Princess
Golden Dawn	Knight	Queen	Prince	Princess
New Golden Dawn	Knight	Queen	Prince	Princess
Motherpeace	Shaman	Priestess	Son	Daughter
Egyptian	Master	Mistress	Warrior	Slave
Connolly	King	Queen	Knight	Princess
Haindl	Father	Mother	Son	Princess
Inner Child	Guardian	Guide	Seeker	Child
Alchemical	King	Queen	Knight	Lady
Oswald Wirth	Roi	Reine	Cavalier	Valet
Spiral	King	Queen	Knight	Princess
Native American	Chief	Matriarch	Warrior	Maiden

ALTERNATE SUIT NAMES

Wands:	Clubs, Staves, Batons, Spears, Rods, Pipes, Scepters
Cups:	Hearts, Goblets, Bowls, Vessels, Crescents, Spheres, Chalices
Swords:	Spades, Arrows, Weapons, Blades
Pentacles:	Diamonds, Coins, Disks, Stones, Shields

Chapter One: The Royal Family

1. E. A. Wallis Budge, *The Gods of the Egyptians,* vol. 1 (New York: Dover Publications, 1969), 3.

2. David Ulansey, "Cultural Transition and Spiritual Transformation: From Alexander the Great to Cyberspace," in *The Vision Thing: Myth, Politics, and Psyche in the World,* ed. Thomas Singer (London; New York: Routledge, 2000), 214.

3. Ibid., 218.

4. Walter Burkert, *Ancient Mystery Cults* (Cambridge: Harvard University Press, 1987), 11.

5. Hans Jonas, *The Gnostic Religion* (Boston: Beacon Press, 1958), 115.

6. Ibid., 56.

7. Walter W. Skeat, *An Etymological Dictionary of the English Language* (Oxford and New York, N.Y.: Oxford University Press, 1958), 139.

8. Joscelyn Godwin, trans., and Adam McLean, commentator, *Salomon Trismosin's "Splendor Solis"* (Grand Rapids, Mich.: Phanes Press, 1991), 34.

9. Papus [Gérard Encausse], *The Tarot of the Bohemians* (1889; reprint, North Hollywood, Calif.: Melvin Powers Wilshire Book Company, 1978), 308.

10. Carl G. Jung, *Psychology and Religion* (New Haven and London: Yale University Press, 1938), 72.

Chapter Two: From Arrow Divination
to a Game of Deputies

1. Catherine Perry Hargrave, *A History of Playing Cards and a Bibliography of Cards and Gaming* (New York: Dover Publications, 1966), 1.

2. Ibid.

3. Maria Leach, ed., *Standard Dictionary of Folklore, Mythology, and Legend* (San Francisco: HarperSanFrancisco, 1972), 135.

4. Hargrave, *History of Playing Cards,* 7.

5. David Parlett, *The Oxford Guide to Card Games* (Oxford and New York, N.Y.: Oxford University Press, 1990), 40.

Chapter Three: Two Hundred Years
of Court Card Interpretation

1. Grimaud's interpretation of the King of Swords as found in Bill Butler, *The Dictionary of the Tarot* (New York: Schocken Books, 1975), 106.

2. Interpretation of the Knight (King) of Swords as found in Angeles Arrien, *The Tarot Handbook* (Sonoma, Calif.: Arcus Publishing, 1987), 107.

3. Butler, *Dictionary of the Tarot,* 38, 104, 54, 78.

4. Papus [Gérard Encausse], *Le Tarot Divinatoire* (Paris: Éditions Dangles, 1973), 145, 138, 124, 131. Translation by the author with the help of Michael D. Bess.

5. Butler, *Dictionary of the Tarot,* 38, 104, 54, 78.

6. Papus, *Tarot of the Bohemians,* 311–14.

7. Arthur E. Waite, *The Pictorial Key to the Tarot* (1910; reprint, New York: University Books, 1959), 254, 228, 174, 204.

8. Eden Gray, *A Complete Guide to the Tarot* (New York: Bantam Books, 1970), 144, 122, 80, 98.

9. Paul Foster Case, *A Course on Tarot Divination* (1933; reprint, Los Angeles: Builders of the Adytum, 1995), 37, 30, 15, 24.

10. Aleister Crowley, *The Book of Thoth* (York Beach, Maine.: Samuel Weiser, 1969), 164, 161, 153, 157.

11. Lon Milo DuQuette, *Tarot of Ceremonial Magick* (York Beach, Maine.: Samuel Weiser, 2001), 112, 106, 92, 102.

12. Arrien, *Tarot Handbook,* 137.

13. Mary K. Greer, *Tarot for Your Self* (North Hollywood, Calif.: Newcastle Publishing, 1984), 234.

Chapter Four: A Qabalistic Equation

1. Carl G. Jung, *The Archetypes and the Collective Unconscious* (New York: Princeton University Press, 1959), 319.

2. Chic Cicero and Sandra Tabatha Cicero, *Self-Initiation into the Golden Dawn Tradition* (Saint Paul: Llewellyn Publications, 1995), 249.

Chapter Six: The Cup Court in the Kingdom of Love

1. Ralph Manheim, trans., *Grimms' Tales for Young and Old* (Garden City, N.Y.: Anchor Press, 1983), 184.

Chapter Eleven: Meditation and the Court Cards

1. William Gray, *Magical Ritual Methods* (York Beach, Maine: Samuel Weiser, 1980), 124.

2. Ibid., 7.

3. Ibid., 126.

4. Dolores Ashcroft-Nowicki, *Highways of the Mind* (Wellingborough, Northamptonshire, England: Aquarian Press, 1987), 18–19.

5. Dolores Ashcroft-Nowicki, *Shining Paths* (Wellingborough, Northamptonshire: Aquarian Press, 1983), 12.

Glossary

Archetype A primordial pattern, concept, or image that can be found across cultures and over time expressed in dream, art, and myth.

Court card The sixteen people, or royalty, cards of the Tarot deck: king, queen, knight, and page of wands, cups, swords, and pentacles. Court card titles may differ from deck to deck. The interpersonal forces (that is, relationships) correspond to the court cards. They also describe personality characteristics or personas of the querent or of people in the querent's life. In a reading, the court cards relate to inner and outer resources available to help in a given situation.

Decanate Refers to a 10-degree segment of the astrological wheel. Each sign of the zodiac (e.g., Libra) occupies 30 degrees (or three 10-degree segments/decanates) of the total 360 degrees.

Divination The act of seeking guidance or counsel from a divine source through the use of an oracle, such as Tarot cards.

Face cards Another phrase used to describe the court cards. "Face" refers to the royal countenances on these sixteen cards.

Golden Dawn An occult society founded in London, England, in 1886 by Drs. Westcott, Woodfort, and Woodman. The Hermetic Order of the Golden Dawn significantly influenced the Western occult movement of the twentieth century.

I Ching or Book of Changes An ancient Chinese oracle that reflects both Confucianist and Taoist philosophy, although presumably much older than either.

Ipsissimus The highest of ten initiatory grades that are used to denote spiritual advancement in many Western esoteric orders. Each grade refers to a Sephirah on the Tree of Life.

Major arcana The major arcana are the twenty-two cards of the Tarot deck with descriptive titles and numbered with Roman numerals beginning with 0, the Fool, through XXI, the World. The presence of the major arcana, or trump suit, distinguishes a Tarot deck from a regular deck of playing cards. The major arcana depict archetypal energies or transformational forces. These forces feel godlike even though they are expressed through commonplace life events. These events more often than not feel beyond our control or "guided." In a Tarot reading, major arcana cards represent the energy seeking to be expressed or working through the querent. They describe the state or focus of the soul.

Minor arcana The minor arcana are the forty numbered cards (ace through ten) of the Tarot deck, plus the sixteen court cards of the four suits: wands, cups, swords, and pentacles. The intrapsychic forces correspond to the minor arcana. In a reading, they describe our psychological state and current life focus or the more mundane activities of life.

Pathworking A guided meditation that might also be described as an inner magical operation designed to produce change on the inner and outer planes.

Pentacle The pentacle is a magical implement, usually a wooden or metal disk with a painted or engraved pentagram on its surface, although other symbols may be depicted instead. The pentacle symbolizes the magician's power to effect change in the physical realm.

Puer A Latin word meaning child. Within Jungian psychology the *puer aeternus* (the mythical eternal child) signifies an adult whose psychological development has not progressed beyond an adolescent level.

Qabalah The mystical branch of Judaism (Kabbalah) later developed by

Christian esoteric practitioners into what is now a primary teaching tool of the Western Mysteries.

Querent The person who is asking the question of the Tarot.

Reversed When a court card appears upside down in a reading it is called a reversed card. Reversed cards are often read differently than "upright" cards.

Sephirah (plural Sephiroth) One of ten spheres depicted on the Qabalistic Tree of Life each representing a stage in the progression of manifestation from spirit to matter.

Shadow As used in this book, *shadow* refers to a court card's baser, negative, or more undeveloped qualities of expression.

Tarot A deck of seventy-eight cards (twenty-two in the major arcana and fifty-six in the minor arcana) that is commonly used as a tool for divination. In the hands of a good psychic, the Tarot can be used to see past, present, and future life events. The Tarot is less commonly known as a psychological or transpersonal tool. In this mode the Tarot can be used to understand the higher forces, mundane influences, and psychological states acting within an individual. On a wider esoteric level, the Tarot describes human existence and can be used solely for study and meditation in the tradition of the Western Mysteries to gain better understanding of oneself in the context of the greater and largely unseen and mysterious whole.

Tattwa A Hindu system that uses color and geometric shapes to convey the elements and elemental qualities.

Tetragrammaton The Hebrew name of God composed of four letters Yod, Heh, Vau, Heh.

Tree of Life A symbolic diagram used within the Qabalah to depict the energies of creation and the emanation of manifestation.

Trick A trick consists of the cards won during one round of play. At the end of trick-taking card games, the person or team with the most tricks usually wins.

Trump In a game of cards a designated suit that wins (triumphs) over any other suit. For example, if spades were trump and one player played a King of Hearts and another played a Two of Spades, the Two would win because it had trumped the King.

Undine According to the alchemist Paracelsus, an undine is an elemental of the watery realm, similar to a water nymph.

Western Mysteries The esoteric spiritual tradition of Western civilization on par with, for example, yoga traditions of the East. The Western Mystery Tradition encompasses occult sciences such as alchemy, astrology, Qabalah, and the Tarot.

Bibliography

BOOKS

Agrippa, Henry Cornelius. *Three Books of Occult Philosophy*. Saint Paul: Llewellyn Publications, 1995.

Arrien, Angeles. *The Tarot Handbook*. Sonoma, Calif.: Arcus Publishing, 1987.

Ashcroft-Nowicki, Dolores. *Highways of the Mind: The Art and History of Pathworking*. Wellingborough, Northamptonshire, England: Aquarian Press, 1987.

———. *Inner Landscapes: A Journey into Awareness by Pathworking*. Northamptonshire, England: Aquarian Press, 1983.

———. *Shining Paths*. Wellingborough, Northamptonshire, England: Aquarian Press, 1983.

Bardon, Franz. *The Practice of Magical Evocation*. Wuppertal, West Germany: Dieter Rüggeberg, 1970.

Benham, W. Gurney. *Playing Cards: The History and Secrets of the Pack*. London: Spring Books, n.d.

Budge, E. A. Wallis. *Egyptian Magic*. New York: Dover Publications, 1971.

———. *The Gods of the Egyptians*. Vol. 1. New York: Dover Publications, 1969.

Burkert, Walter. *Ancient Mystery Cults*. Cambridge: Harvard University Press, 1987.

Butler, Bill. *The Dictionary of the Tarot*. New York: Schocken Books, 1975.

Butler, W. E. *The Magician, His Training and Work*. North Hollywood, Calif.: Melvin Powers Wilshire Book Company, 1959.

Cad, Irene. *Tarot and Individuation: Correspondences with Cabala and Alchemy*. York Beach, Maine: Nicolas Hays, 1994.

Case, Paul Foster. *A Course on Tarot Divination*. 1933. Reprint, Los Angeles: Builders of the Adytum, 1995.

Christeaan, Aaron, Van Hulle, JP, Clark, M.C. *Michael: The Basic Teachings*. Orinda, Calif.: Michael Educational Foundation, 1990.

Cicero, Chic, and Sandra Tabatha Cicero. *Self-Initiation into the Golden Dawn Tradition*. Saint Paul: Llewellyn Publications, 1995.

Crowley, Aleister. *The Book of Thoth*. 1944. Reprint, York Beach, Maine: Samuel Weiser, 1969.

Douglas, Alfred. *The Tarot*. London: Penguin Books, 1972.

Drury, Nevill. *Inner Visions: Explorations in Magical Consciousness*. London: Arcana, 1979.

DuQuette, Lon Milo. *The Chicken Qabalah of Rabbi Lamed Ben Clifford*. York Beach, Maine: Samuel Weiser, 2001.

———. *Tarot of Ceremonial Magick*. York Beach, Maine: Samuel Weiser, 1995.

Fairfield, Gail. *Everyday Tarot*. Boston: Weiser Books, 2002.

Fortune, Dion. *The Mystical Qabalah*. York Beach, Maine: Samuel Weiser, 1984.

Godwin, Joscelyn, trans., and Adam McLean, commentator. *Salomon Trismosin's "Splendor Solis."* Grand Rapids, Mich.: Phanes Press, 1991.

Gray, Eden. *A Complete Guide to the Tarot*. New York: Bantam Books, 1970.

Gray, William. *Magical Ritual Methods*. York Beach, Maine: Samuel Weiser, 1980.

Greer, Mary K. *The Complete Book of Tarot Reversals*. Saint Paul: Llewellyn Publications, 2002.

———. *Tarot Constellations*. North Hollywood, Calif.: Newcastle Publishing, 1987.

———. *Tarot for Your Self*. North Hollywood, Calif.: Newcastle Publishing, 1984.

———. *Tarot Mirrors*. North Hollywood, Calif.: Newcastle Publishing, 1988.

Gwain, Rose. *Discovering Your Self through the Tarot: A Jungian Guide to Archetypes and Personality*. Rochester, Vt.: Destiny Books, 1994.

Hargrave, Catherine Perry. *A History of Playing Cards and a Bibliography of Cards and Gaming*. New York: Dover Publications, 1966.

Hoffman, Edward. *The Way of Splendor: Jewish Mysticism and Modern Psychology*. Northvale, N.J.: Jason Aronson, 1981.

Jette, Christine. *Tarot Shadow Work: Using the Dark Shadows to Heal*. Saint Paul: Llewellyn Publications, 2001.

Johnson, Robert. *Inner Work*. San Francisco: HarperSanFrancisco, 1986.

Jonas, Hans. *The Gnostic Religion*. Boston: Beacon Press, 1958.

Jung, Carl G. *The Archetypes and the Collective Unconscious*. New York: Princeton University Press, 1959.

———. *Psychology and Religion*. New Haven and London: Yale University Press, 1938.

Kaplan, Stuart R. *The Encyclopedia of Tarot*. Vols. 1–3. Stamford, Conn: U.S. Games Systems, 1978.

Kliegman, Isabel Radow. *Tarot and the Tree of Life: Finding Everyday Wisdom in the Minor Arcana*. Wheaton, Ill.: Theosophical Publishing House, 1997.

Knight, Gareth. *Magical World of the Tarot: Fourfold Mirror of the Universe*. York Beach, Maine: Samuel Weiser, 1991.

———. *Practical Guide to Qabalistic Symbolism*. York Beach, Maine: Samuel Weiser, 1965.

———. *Tarot and Magic: Images for Rituals and Pathworkings*. Rochester, Vt.: Destiny Books, 1986.

Leach, Maria, ed. *Standard Dictionary of Folklore, Mythology, and Legend*. San Francisco: HarperSanFrancisco, 1972.

Lévi, Eliphas. *Transcendental Magic*. 1856. Reprint, York Beach, Maine: Samuel Weiser, 1972.

Manheim, Ralph, trans. *Grimms' Tales for Young and Old*. Garden City, N.Y.: Anchor Press, 1983.

Mathers, S. L. MacGregor. *The Tarot*. 1888. Reprint, York Beach, Maine: Samuel Weiser, 1969.

McLean, Adam. *The Alchemical Mandala*. Grand Rapids, Mich.: Phanes Press, 1989.

Naydler, Jeremy. *Temple of the Cosmos: The Ancient Egyptian Experience of the Sacred*. Rochester, Vt.: Inner Traditions, 1996.

Noble, Vicki. *Motherpeace: A Way to the Goddess through Myth, Art, and Tarot*. San Francisco: Harper and Row, 1983.

Papus [Gerard Encausse]. *Le Tarot Divinatoire*. Paris: Éditions Dangles, 1973.

———. *The Tarot of the Bohemians*. 1889. Reprint, North Hollywood, Calif.: Melvin Powers Wilshire Book Company, 1978.

Parlett, David. *The Oxford Guide to Card Games*. Oxford and New York, N.Y.: Oxford University Press, 1990.

Peach, Emily. *The Tarot Workbook*. Northamptonshire, England: Aquarian Press, 1984.

Pollack, Rachel. *Seventy-eight Degrees of Wisdom: Part 2, The Minor Arcana and Readings*. London: Thorsons, 1983.

Regardie, Israel. *The Golden Dawn*. Saint Paul: Llewellyn Publications, 1971.

———. *The Middle Pillar*. Saint Paul: Llewellyn Publications, 1988.

Rosengarten, Arthur. *Tarot and Psychology: Spectrums of Possibility.* Saint Paul: Paragon House, 2000.

Skeat, Walter W. *An Etymological Dictionary of the English Language.* Oxford and New York, N.Y.: Oxford University Press, 1958.

Stevens, José, and Simon Warwick-Smith. *The Michael Handbook.* Sonoma, Calif: Warwick Press, 1987.

Sykes, Bryan. *The Seven Daughters of Eve.* New York: W. W. Norton, 2001.

Tilley, Roger. *A History of Playing Cards.* New York: Clarkson N. Potter, 1973.

Ulansey, David. "Cultural Transition and Spiritual Transformation: From Alexander the Great to Cyberspace." In *The Vision Thing: Myth, Politics, and Psyche in the World,* edited by Thomas Singer. London; New York: Routledge, 2000.

Waite, Arthur E. *The Pictorial Key to the Tarot.* 1910. Reprint, New York: University Books, 1959.

Walker, Barbara G. *The Secrets of the Tarot: Origin, History, and Symbolism.* San Francisco: HarperSanFrancisco, 1984.

Wang, Robert. *An Introduction to the Golden Dawn Tarot.* York Beach, Maine: Samuel Weiser, 1978.

———. *The Qabalistic Tarot.* York Beach, Maine: Samuel Weiser, 1983.

Wanless, James. *New Age Tarot: Guide to the Thoth Deck.* Carmel, Calif.: Merrill-West Publishing, 1986.

Wanless, James, and Angeles Arrien, eds. *Wheel of Tarot: A New Revolution.* Carmel, Calif.: Merrill-West Publishing, 1992.

Wilhelm, Richard, and Cary F. Baynes, trans. *The I Ching or Book of Changes.* New York: Princeton University Press, 1950.

Wing, R. L. *The Illustrated "I Ching."* Garden City, N.Y.: Dolphin Books, Doubleday, 1982.

Wowk, Kathleen. *Playing Cards of the World.* Guildford, Surrey: Lutterworth Press, 1983.

WEB SITES CONSULTED

www.pagat.com The Web site of the International Playing-Card Society. Articles consulted: "Card Games in Italy," "Unsolved Problems in Playing-Card Research," "History of Playing-Cards."

www.tarotsociety.org The Web site of the International Tarot Society. Article consulted: "Eden Gray Dies at 97."

http://jducoeur.org/game-hist/game-recon-tarot.html Medieval and Renaissance Games home page. Article consulted: "Game Report: Early French Tarot.

www.tarock.net A Tarock Web site. Article consulted: "Tarock Rules."

www.villarevak.org A Tarot Web site by James W. Revak. Articles consulted: "The TarotL History Information Sheet," "Etteilla: The First Professional Tarotist," "Tarot Divination: Three Parallel Traditions."

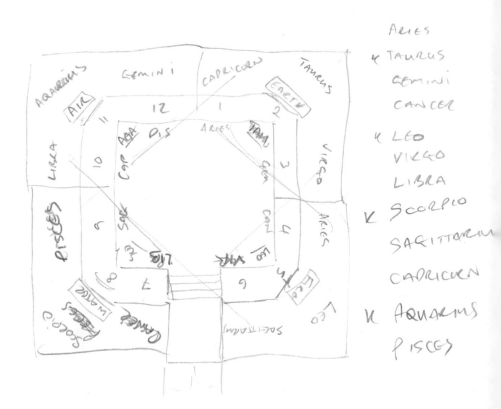